WHY EXECUTION FAILS

AND WHAT TO DO ABOUT IT

2nd Edition

John Fortin

WHY EXECUTION FAILS

AND WHAT TO DO ABOUT IT

2nd Edition

John W. Fortin, CMRP

ISBN 978-1-941872-80-2
HF042019

Printed in the United States of America.

Publisher: Reliabilityweb.com
Design and Layout: Jocelyn Brown

For information: Reliabilityweb.com
www.reliabilityweb.com
8991 Daniels Center Drive, Suite 105, Ft. Myers, FL 33912
Toll Free: 888-575-1245 | Phone: 239-333-2500
E-mail: crm@reliabilityweb.com

10 9 8 7 6 5 4 3 2

Dedication

To my mom and dad,
Barbara and Dennis Fortin.

Table of Contents

Acknowledgments

First, a thank you to Terrence O'Hanlon who encouraged me to start writing. And then pinned an "Author" pendant on my International Maintenance Conference badge shortly thereafter! He was truly excited as recent studies by Reliabilityweb.com and others clearly indicate the significant need for a guidebook for successful change by someone who has lived it and has helped others build sustainable programs.

To my wife Trish and daughters Samantha and Sydney – they supported my long hours working and traveling to help clients successfully execute change initiatives. They have not seen, but believe! If you read this book, maybe you will begin to understand and be able to finally explain to family and friends what I actually do.

To my friends who welcomed me to the CH2M community – Scott Haskins, Elisa Speranza, John Rogers, Roop Lutchman, Karen Kovolo and those who helped me advance my thinking – a big thank you. And to the Massachusetts Water Resources Authority's award-winning team listed in this book's Appendix A case study who helped me "develop and pilot test" the DELTA FORCE principles for successful execution – all which stand true today!

And finally, last but not least, to all the asset management and reliability professionals I have worked with along the way. Of particular note, thank you Biju George, Jim Oldach, Jake Peck, Kevin Campanella, John Shinn, Eric Stevens, Danny Beaudoin, Tyler Richards, Jeff Boss, Clint Davis, Sam Paske and Craig Edlund for your creative thinking, use of the model elements and encouragement to continue in the quest for implementation excellence.

Introduction

Industry studies have documented that approximately seventy percent of change initiatives fail to deliver expectations. Over the years, and even more recently, top-down and bottom-up leadership has struggled to make improvement programs take hold. In the midst of every effort, there are typically three basic components: people, process and technology. How well each of these interact with each other is where efficiency and effectiveness can be measured. While it appears to be very simple, employees are already stretched thin, given economic pressures and the constant drive to do more with less.

With every new initiative, the office hallways echo with, "Here it comes again, another flavor of the month program – ugh!" In the drive for a competitive advantage and trying to leverage technologies as key efficiency components, companies launch improvement efforts on a regular basis. Strategic plans are commonplace and typically include a variety of cross-cutting initiatives and activities. In the whirlwind of normal workloads and the excitement to launch, executives and managers can forget to establish an execution strategy – a leading root cause of the high failure rate of implementation efforts!

In this revised edition, there is an added focus on the executive sponsor role. As a key stakeholder for supporting corporate initiatives, there is little to no guidance or training provided for this role. The new Chapter 4 titled "The ART of Executive Sponsorship" promises to provide a robust framework that will help formalize and operationalize this critical role to coordinate, own and drive change efforts to successful completion.

It should be clearly understood that there is no "silver bullet" solution nor a straight line trajectory to completion. The world we live in is constantly changing and there most likely will be course correction needs along the implementation phase. Be prepared to accept and adapt to these dynamics and shifts because they will occur!

The DELTA FORCE model for execution excellence is built on over eighteen years of proven success helping companies and executives accelerate and deliver real value from technical initiatives, such as asset performance and reliability management change initiatives. The concepts are simple and the model has been developed to help identify and simplify the various components. DELTA focuses on successful execution process steps and FORCE provides execution imperatives, sometimes referred to as critical success factors. In short, the DELTA FORCE's model has been developed to close the gap, accelerate change and deliver return on investment (ROI).

This book is written around the proven execution excellence elements and is supplemented with real-life stories and anecdotes that have helped shape the DELTA FORCE model.

Chapter 1
The Need for Execution Excellence

As evidenced, Figure 1-1 validates past and present research that, in many cases, up to seventy percent of change efforts and new strategies fail to create a sustained result. This is a paradox because most effective strategies and techniques are well-known and documented. The costs for improvement programs are significant and company executives demand return on investment, so the need for execution excellence is of paramount importance. In the world of asset performance and reliability, there are technical frameworks that help define "what" should be included in such an improvement effort. Often, the missing link is "how" to effect *sustainable* change.

Frameworks, such as the ISO55000 Standards for Asset Management and Reliabilityweb.com's Uptime® Elements™, provide the industry with a breakdown of technical components necessary for a comprehensive asset and reliability program. Related training and certification programs also provide knowledge and tools mainly focused on technical aspects. Of the three basic components (people, process and technology) that make up change efforts, these models mainly focus on two of the three – process and technology. They leave out the critical component – people.

The DELTA FORCE model encompasses all three, with a real focus on the people aspect. This has led companies to achieve significant return on their investment and sustained change. See Appendix A for a case study in which many of the aspects of this execu-

Figure 1-1: Success Rate for Implementing Change

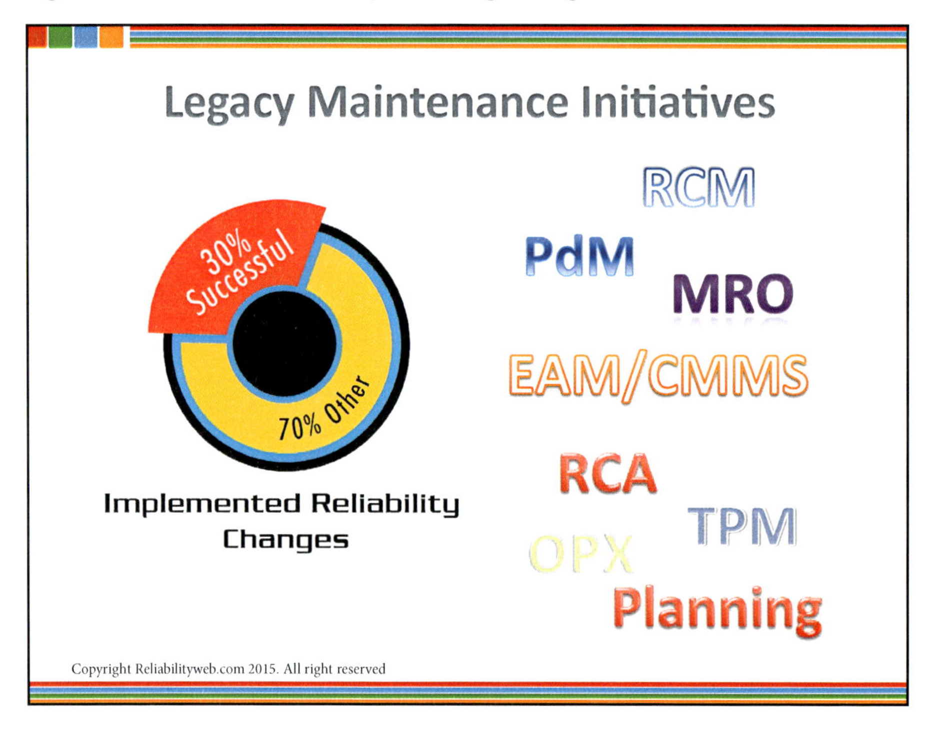

tion excellence concept were first applied and tested. Over time, further refinements have been made through both successful and unsuccessful programs. In all cases, the technical components have been the easiest and the people components the most challenging. This has been true for each and every industry and geography. While many believe they are unique or different, there are many similarities and each can learn from the other to save valuable time and resources.

Chapter 2
The DELTA FORCE Model

The DELTA FORCE model for execution excellence is built on many years of proven success helping companies and executives accelerate and deliver real value from asset performance and reliability management change initiatives. The concepts are simple and the model has been developed to help identify and simplify the various components. The DELTA part of the acronym focuses on successful plan development process steps and the FORCE acronym provides imperatives that should be considered critical success factors during implementation of the plan. This overview summarizes the model.

The DELTA Strategic Planning Process

- **D**efine the Problem/Opportunity
- **E**nvision the Future
- **L**ead by Example
- **T**ask Management
- **A**ctive Monitoring

The FORCE Strategic Plan Execution Imperatives:

- **F**ollow-through – On actions and activities
- **O**rganized – Treat the initiative as a capital project
- **R**espect among team members
- **C**ulture awareness
- **E**ntrepreneurial spirit encouraged

Figure 2-1: DELTA Strategic Planning Process

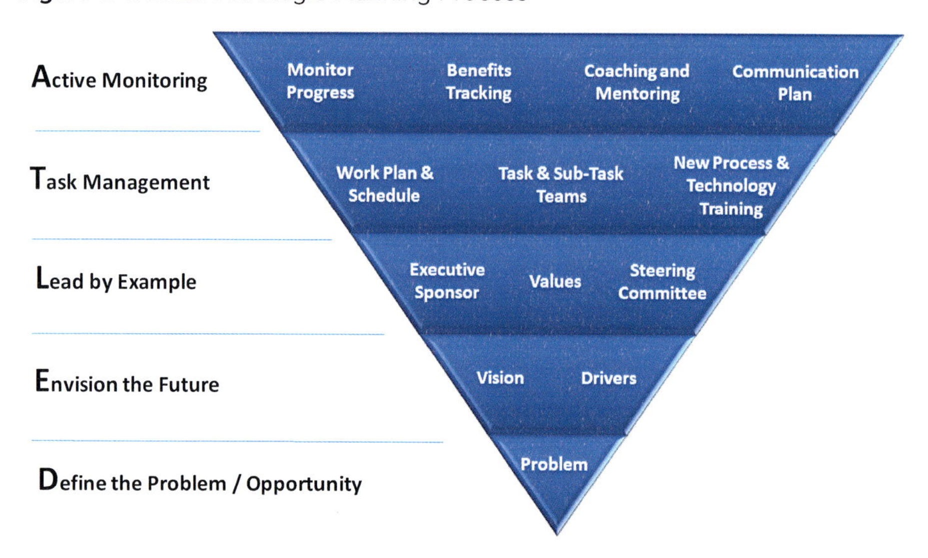

Here's a more detailed explanation of the DELTA FORCE model.

The DELTA strategic planning process should be utilized when senior leadership desires to move from a current or status quo status to a new, more improved, efficient and effective status and revised processes. Outside facilitation services can be the most effective approach to executing effective change management programs. DELTA is a combination of proven methodologies that can help transform any organization. Figure 2-1 depicts the elements of the DELTA process that are further detailed here and in the following chapters.

Define the Problem/Opportunity – This is the first step where senior leadership defines an improvement initiative that is needed to remain safe, competitive, efficient, or some similar driver for change.

Envision the Future – In this second step, the organization's senior leadership reviews the mission statement, drivers for change and expected outcomes, and then develop a vision statement (i.e., future state). This visioning process is critical as it sets the foundation for the goals, strategies and activities that will be required to move to the future state.

Lead by Example – This next step is where a series of leadership activities are initiated and required to continue throughout the life of the change effort. An executive sponsor needs to be identified and designated the senior leadership's corporate sponsor to champion and guide the program through completion. This individual should be respected by peers, have the ability to focus on results and have good communications skills. See Chapter 4, which outlines "The ART of Executive Sponsorship," providing a formal framework for this critical role to help select and guide this person to own and drive change efforts. A steering committee of cross-functional leaders needs to be formerly chartered to help lead and support the change implementation efforts. Together, the executive sponsor and steering committee will define operating and values statements.

Task Management – The fourth step is for the steering team, comprised of key stakeholders, to establish a work plan to help move to the envisioned state. Outside facilitation and subject matter experts may be desired to complete this task in a timely manner. Together, the group should define a set of four to six goal statements. Each goal statement will contain supporting initiative/strategy statements, along with individual activities or tasks. Once this is complete, the work plan should be prioritized and a completion schedule established. The work prioritization should be a risk-based process and include any foundational type activities as top priority. Chapter 5 further details the team-based implementation model that can be leveraged when comprehensive strategic initiatives should be completed by cross-functional task teams to solve the more cross-departmental and often more complex changes. Each task team should be established with a formal team charter. Teams will typically create new processes, update or add technology/tools that may require structural/organizational changes, and documentation and training on new procedures. See Appendix D, which provides example team charters.

Active Monitoring – The fifth step is about project management. A regular steering committee meeting schedule should be established (e.g., monthly) to monitor and reward each team's progress against charters and scheduled work activities. During these meetings,

Figure 2-2: Knowledge Transfer

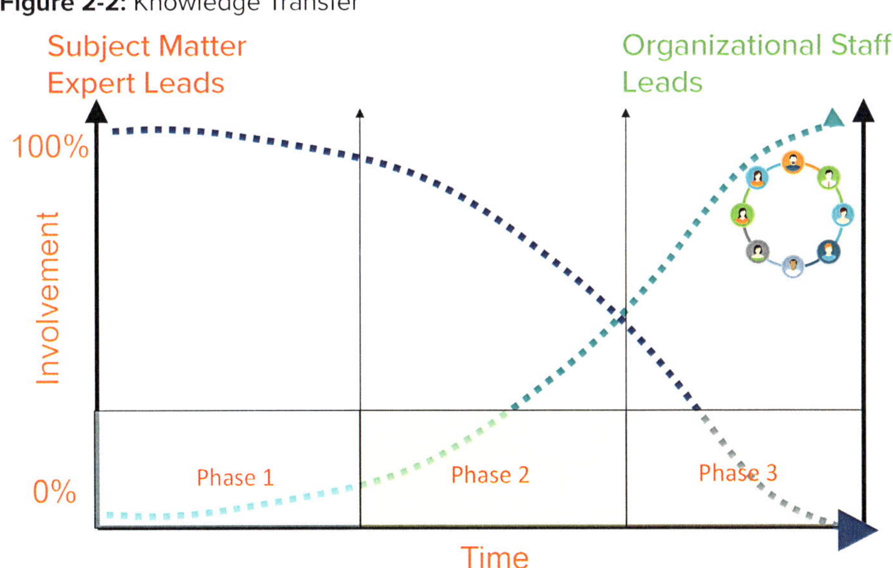

progress, as well as issues, are discussed for timely resolution. In addition, there needs to be a formal effort put forth to reward/acknowledge achievements and document positive changes and benefits; including tangible (e.g., financial) and intangible (e.g., improved skills, morale). Chapter 6 provides more details on elements of a formal communications plan, which is a very important component to help keep the organization well-informed on status and benefits. The plan should target both internal and external stakeholders and include a variety of methods, such as all-staff meetings/memos, newsletter articles and information boards. If there are a variety of task teams working concurrently on activities, a regular presentation forum to the steering committee and executive management team is another means to communicate progress across teams. In many cases, change initiatives are multi-year efforts, so the continued use of internal/external coaching and mentoring with knowledge transfer plans have proven successful in sustaining the change momentum. A budget also should be allocated for such support. Figure 2-2 shows how knowledge transfer could occur between subject matter experts and organizational staff members over a period of time, such as multi-phased projects.

The FORCE strategic execution excellence imperatives are used in concert with the DELTA model as a way to establish critical success factors for the program and supporting projects. It is important to combine these principles with the DELTA model to help accelerate change and deliver ROI. Figure 2-3 depicts the elements of the FORCE imperatives that are further detailed here and in the following chapters.

Figure 2-3: FORCE Strategic Plan Execution Imperatives

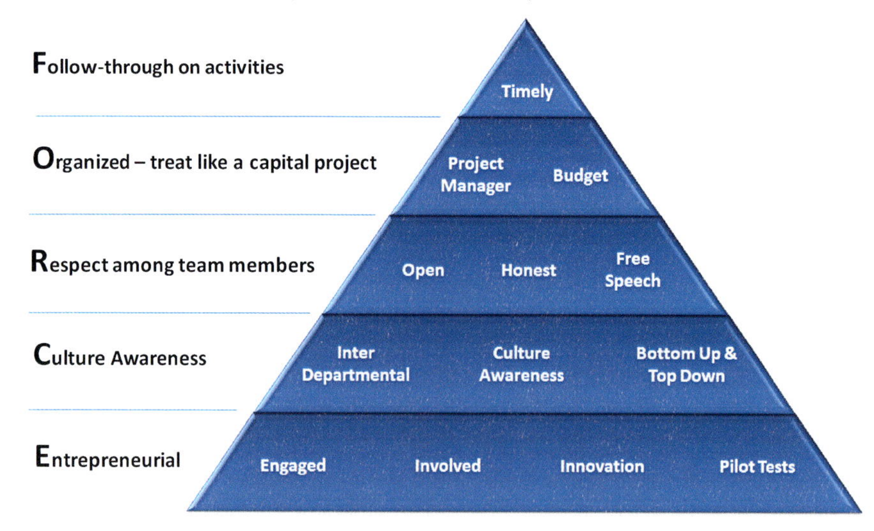

Follow-through – Change projects typically overlap with existing duties, so for timely change, the organization's supervisors need to understand that some workloads may need to be shifted or external resources required. Steering and task team members will be required to attend additional meetings, workshops and training, and may also receive to-do activities in addition to their current responsibilities. This should be handled through meeting management best practices that include the use of meeting agendas and minutes. They will need time to complete these assignments and come prepared for each team meeting/session. Finally, and maybe most importantly, senior leadership needs to ensure that the organization only engages in a reasonable amount of concurrent change initiatives to avoid resource strain. A worthwhile exercise is to review annual corporate strategic plan projects and initiatives against functional group resource impacts. See Appendix E for meeting management templates.

Organized – Change initiatives typically include people, processes and technology changes. They can be successful and sustainable only if handled in an organized manner, similar to the way a capital construction project is managed with a project manager, clearly defined scope, schedule and multi-year budget. The use of a team collaboration software tool or other document management tools can provide a way to minimize the need for quality control and ongoing e-mail exchanges.

Respect among team members – When it comes to change, one colleague always notes that, "Everyone is on a different part of the journey." So, it is important for leadership and team members to be mindful and respectful of that. Team concepts work best if the atmosphere encourages team members to be open, honest and allows them to speak freely and constructively to help advance the group's mission. Group sessions are typically good models for change, but not all individuals function well in this setting. Setting aside individual time with team members can be a respectful way for leadership to engage and encourage involvement and feedback.

Culture awareness – Each organization has a set of inherent behaviors and values and being mindful of these is important. In many cases, organizations are trying to change a behavior (e.g., rewarding reactivity). Awareness of top-down versus bottom-up change approaches can be helpful in designing work plans. Use of interdepartmental teams also can be a good approach to minimizing group culture/behavioral concerns. Initiative executive sponsors and leadership should focus on aligning team requirements with individual member strengths to set them up for success. Mentorship and formal succession planning are two operating principles that can advance and sustain cultural shifts. Understanding the behaviors and how they impact a change initiative and its outcomes is a worthy exercise that can help prepare leadership, shape team membership and determine activities in the communications and work plans.

Entrepreneurial spirit – It is important to have a good initiative work plan and schedule, but it is also important to use them as a guideline, allowing for flexibility and individual engagement and innovation. The saying, "involvement breeds commitment" is a true statement when it comes to meaningful engagement from people in the change effort. Steering and other team leaders need to foster a sense of individual entrepreneurship in solving complex problems. And the plan needs to include time and the budget to celebrate successes/wins to establish and build momentum and a strong sense of teamwork. It is good to adopt the "no idea is a bad one" concept, however, this is an area where respect will need to be enforced to ensure open individual input. Chapter 7 provides details on the iDEA process, which can be employed to maximize each contribution by following a simple four-step process: individual input – discuss – evaluate – act (yes, modify, no). The use of pilot testing concepts prior to full-scale rollout is another proven method for new ideas/approaches. Finally, senior leadership needs to proactively manage workload spread so the typical go-to staff is not overburdened. This approach will help ensure timelier project completion, cultural alignment and sustainment of change initiatives.

The DELTA FORCE Model Lifecycle View

Another way to view the DELTA FORCE model is through a strategic initiative's lifecycle. As shown in Figure 2-4, there is a need to understand the FORCE elements' roles and impacts on the DELTA process during the project's execution phase. As previously noted, the FORCE elements should be considered as critical success factors for successful strategy execution.

Figure 2-4: The Delta FORCE Model Lifecycle View

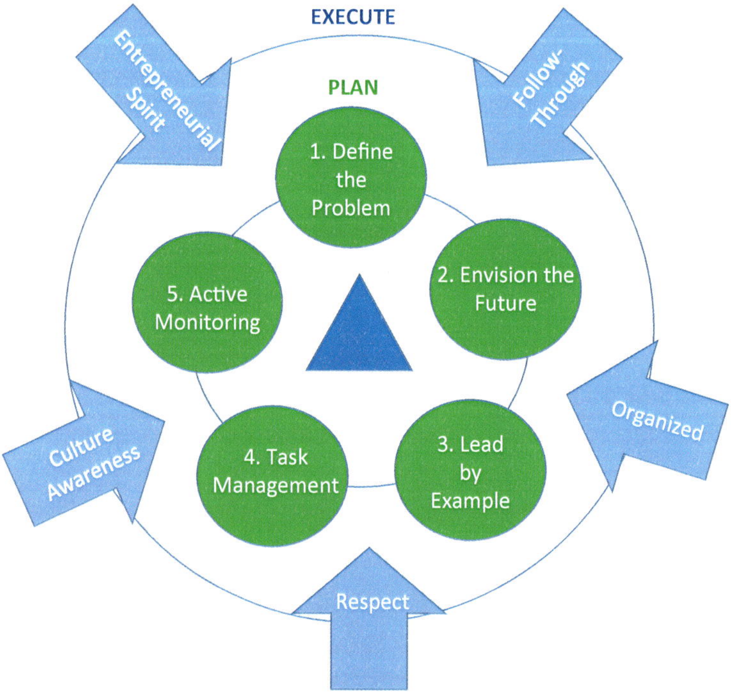

Chapter 3

Developing the Strategic Plan

As described in the "D" of DELTA, defining the problem/opportunity is the first important step. It is most effective if the problem/opportunity statement is supported by a high-level initiative documented in the company's annual corporate strategic plan. For example, a large water utility company preparing to launch a comprehensive asset management program listed it in its annual strategic plan as initiative #24 with the goal to plan, manage and coordinate the engineering, maintenance, operations and financing required to maintain all facilities to regulatory requirements. High-level corporate initiatives typically will receive some resource allocations, including an executive sponsor held accountable to execute a schedule and budget for implementation. So either an initiative already exists or there is a driver for change that requires one to be formulated. In either case, there needs to be a few key foundational elements to support successful and sustainable execution.

A variety of methods can help define the initiative(s). In the case of asset performance and reliability management, a formal gap or needs assessment can be completed to compare the organization against industry best practices frameworks, such as Uptime Elements (Figure 3-1), the ISO55000 Standards for Asset Management, and related industry benchmarking projects. Another more simplified approach is completing a strengths, weaknesses, opportunities and threats (SWOT) assessment. It is important to investigate the available framework that will best align

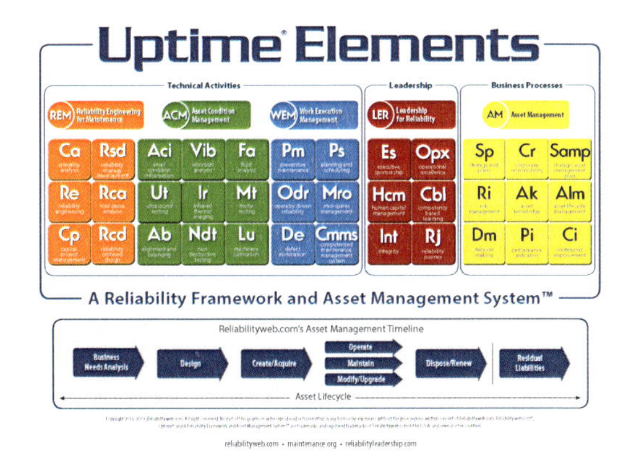

Figure 3-1: Uptime Elements Framework

with the organization and its culture. There are high-level or very tactical type assessment survey formats. One needs to consider corporate leadership's threshold for moderate or extensive change, mid-level management's ability to handle change, along with routine work activities and other critical success factors. The approach and method used are only a means to an end – to help identify gaps and a strategic plan to help close the gaps.

Figure 3-2: The Strategic Planning Process

As shown in Figure 3-2, the strategic planning process should be led and supported by an executive sponsor and include some degree of a business case evaluation (BCE) process to justify the change investment in the eyes of all stakeholders. Depending on the size and scale of the initiative, the plan development should always include cross-functional representation from all key stakeholder groups. In the case of asset and reliability management, this includes all functions that impact the lifecycle of the system or facility, including departments such as operations, maintenance, engineering, finance, procurement and technology. Chapter 4 provides more guidance on the attributes, roles and top modes of success (ART), but in simple terms, the executive sponsor should be respected by peers, have the ability to focus on results and have good communications skills.

Figure 3-3 outlines the basic strategic plan elements and linkages to desired results. It can be organized into a series of cascading elements that connect the mission and vision

Figure 3-3: Strategic Plan Elements and Linkages

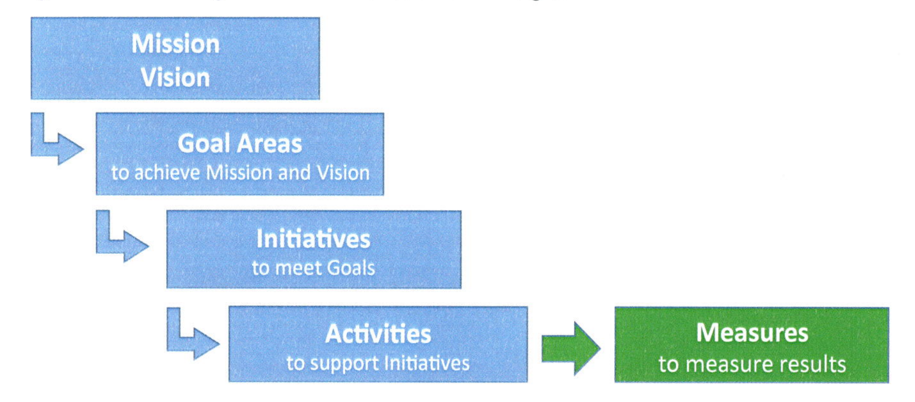

to goals, initiatives and activities. These then need to be managed like a project, with ongoing performance measurements and follow-through. See Appendix B for a sample worksheet used for building a strategic plan.

Developing mission and vision statements as part of a "visioning" phase are very important components to execution and sustainability. Simply pulling the current ones from the corporate boardroom's walls is not an option. Each initiative has its own particular statements that should certainly *support* the corporate version and be referenced during its development. A variety of ways exist to develop mission (what we do) and vision (where we want to go) statements. Some of these also include values (how we will treat each other) and operating principles (how we will work together to deliver this project). The most important aspect is for the development to be done by a group of key stakeholders with cross-functional and top-down/bottom-up representation. Sustainable change typically impacts many groups, so to be successful, it needs to have involvement and engagement across the board. It is okay to bring examples of these documents to the group as a way to jump-start the process. But a fatal flaw can happen if the executive sponsor comes to the stakeholder group with these already completed for approval signatures in a single meeting. The development of effective mission and vision statements requires a series of meetings and workshops so each stakeholder has a fingerprint on the document. Figure 3-4 is from an award-winning utility company that created a strategic plan summary for communications purposes that included mission, vision and values statements, and goal areas for a two-year maintenance reliability improvement initiative. In another example at a large industrial company, an effort to more strongly unify the group challenged the steering team to have fun and come up with a name for the team and its improvement

Figure 3-4: Sample Mission, Vision, Values and Strategic Plan Summary

Mission Preserve process functions so we protect the health of the citizens and the quality of our environment
Vision Maximize plant throughput – treatment, at the most effective cost
Values Honesty, Accountability, Integrity and Respect

2012-2013

Strategic Maintenance & Reliability Plan

Goals and Objectives:

1. Focus on Core Business Prevent and correct failures. Reduce special projects.
2. Training Invest in maintenance and reliability program and specialized training.
3. Communication Increase involvement and awareness through leadership listening.
4. Reliability Generate proactive work through improved maintenance strategies and a living program to improve uptime.
5. Maintainability Reduce downtime through centralized and decentralized predictive maintenance program.
6. Plan and Schedule Planner/Scheduler are focused on future work and capturing work history.

initiaitve. The result helped bring the team closer together as a leading body, but team members also created a tagline that gave meaning to their initiative's vision. The team was named Steering Committee for Operational Reliability Excellence (SCORE) and its vision was to achieve Maintenance, Operational and Reliability Excellence (MORE).

Chapter 4
The ART of Executive Sponsorship™

The success of any corporate strategic initiative is usually linked to strong executive sponsorship. In any large and complex organization, some people at every level of the organization will not be convinced that asset management and reliability programs provide value, is affordable or view such efforts as simply "the flavor of the month." A well-placed, articulate and influential sponsor has the unique ability to both motivate and compel teams to support a new strategic investment. The executive sponsor leading the effort needs to be a passionate advocate, believing that asset management and reliability is an imperative – an imperative based on a powerful business case evaluation (BCE) that justifies the investment. The sooner an organization can find a strong executive sponsor, the better positioned they will be for timely success and a strong return on investment (ROI).

Recently, organizations have been asking about executive sponsorship including questions such as:

1. What makes a good executive sponsor?
2. What are their responsibilities?
3. How do they actively and successfully support the project execution phase?

In response to these, and as depicted in Figure 4-1, this chapter introduces a unique focus on the "**L**" component within DELTA, which represents "**L**eadership." Providing a deeper dive, the **ART** of Executive Sponsorship™

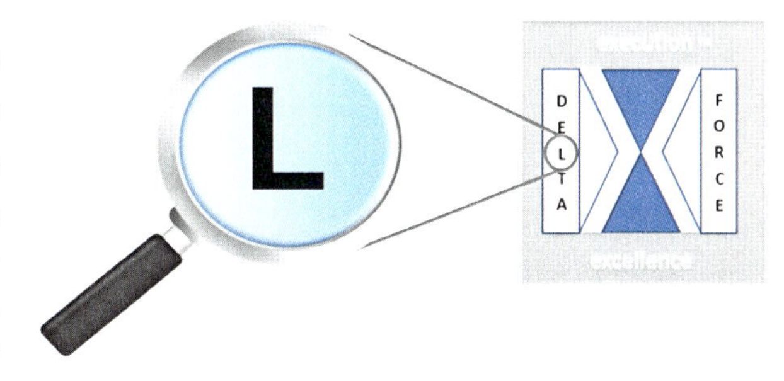

Figure 4-1: Focus on Leadership

framework helps define critical success factors in selecting and executing executive sponsorship (i.e., who, what and how):

- ✓ **A**ttributes of an effective sponsor,
- ✓ **R**esponsibilities definition, and establishes the
- ✓ **T**op 5 modes for success

The "**Attributes"** of Executive Sponsorship can be characterized as qualities such as:

- Good understanding of how the business operates and of the corporate strategy
- True stakeholder, can have a fundamental impact on the organization's performance
- Respected by peers with power to influence/impact success, overcome resistance
- In a position to authorize resources (short and long-term)
- Ability to provide guidelines to shape team decision-making at all levels
- Ability to envision the future state
- Models and shapes others' behaviors
- Good communicator and storyteller with ability to motivate in good and bad times
- Organized but not a micromanager
- Availability to coach and mentor teams from kickoff to closure

The "**Responsibilities"** of Executive Sponsorship can be defined as:

- Responsible for the business case evaluation (BCE) justification and overall success of the initiative
- Goal alignment and communication with executive peers (often referred to as the C-Suite), coordination with other company initiatives that may require the same staff resources
- Responsible for team member selection (including removal/additions)
- Secure resources (funding, staff availability, outside support)
- Provide direction via team chartering and helps define critical success and risk factors
- Completes "Execution Readiness" and "Execution Success Status" scorecard reviews including analysis of results (i.e., risks) and follow-up actions
- Responsible for securing steering team buy-in
- Assures accountability, quality and timeliness of deliverables
- Creates an environment where candid and honest dialog is the norm, challenges status quo and assists in conflict resolution
- Establishes working relationship "guidelines" with project manager who manages scope, schedule, budget and deliverables
- Coordinate recognition/celebration of team work efforts success

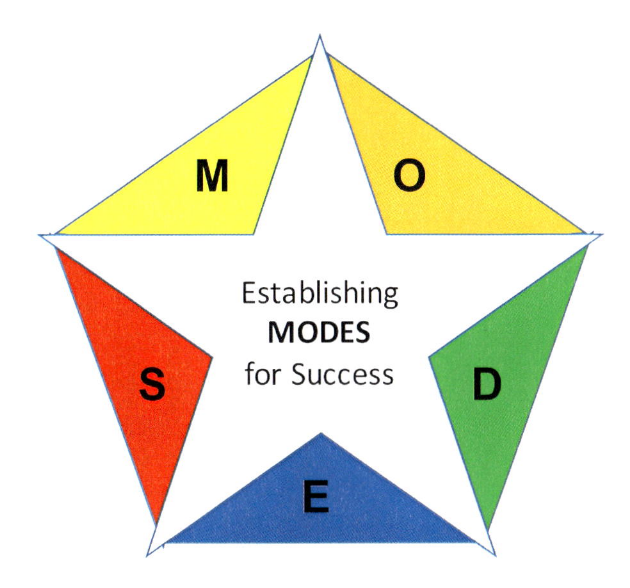

Figure 4-2: Establishing MODES for Success

As shown in Figure 4-2, the **"Top 5 Modes for Success"** for Executive Sponsorship is built around the success **MODES** model on how to be an effective executive sponsor:

Manage Cross-Functional Alignment – with executive peers, coordination with other initiatives, helps set the mission/vision/values statements, communicates project value/status top-down/bottom-up

Ownership of the Business Case for Change – develops and owns the business case evaluation (BCE) documentation with the project manager to justify the investment

Direction and Leadership – charters steering team, establishes and monitors critical success factors, active and visible sponsorship

Encouragement and Resourcing – motivates and provides team with open/honest/immediate feedback, assures resources are available to teams

Sustainment and Risk Management – supports team member selection, owns the "Execution Readiness Review" and "Execution Success Status Review" scorecards, participates in managing risks identified in these exercises

The ART of Executive Sponsorship™ 5-Step Process Model

One way to articulate the roll-up of activities of the executive sponsor is to simplify it into the 5-Step Process model. As shown in Figure 4-3, this covers a project or initiative's lifecycle from identification of the strategic initiative to selecting the most appropriate executive sponsor through to the BCE, team selection, execution and project wrap-up.

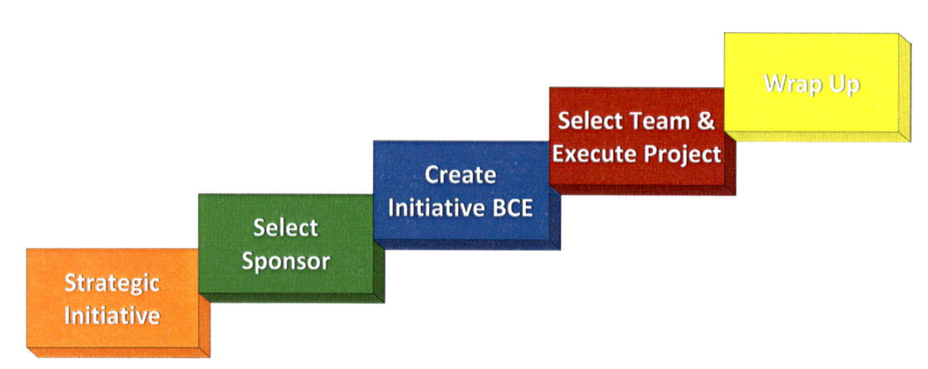

Figure 4-3: The Executive Sponsorship 5-Step Process

The 5-Step Process model provides a simple framework that can assist executive leaders in selecting the right sponsor and creating an easy-to-follow involvement checklist for success.

Step 1 – Strategic Initiative Identification

As discussed in Chapter 2, the D in DELTA is to define the problem or opportunity, which is later converted into strategic initiatives and/or projects. These are often needed to help organizations remain safe, competitive, efficient or some other driver for change. As noted in Chapter 3, there are a variety of tools to help organizations formally understand the needs for change such as: strategic planning sessions, gap assessments, strengths/weaknesses/opportunities/threats (SWOT) analyses and industry benchmarking. From such efforts, improvement initiatives develop that will now require an executive sponsor to shape and execute.

Tools Summary:

- Strategic Planning
- Gap/Needs Assessment
- SWOT Analysis
- Industry Benchmarking

Step 2 – Select the Executive Sponsor

Since this is a critical function, there needs to be a bit more rigor in the identification and selection of the most appropriate senior leader in the organization to fulfill this role. As noted above, the framework is called The **ART** of Executive Sponsorship™, which provides the **A**ttributes and **R**oles to identify the best candidate. The **T**op 5 modes of success then create an easy-to-follow involvement checklist of activities that will provide guidance through the life of the project. Once candidates have been considered, there is now a tool available to help assess their abilities. Appendix C includes the Executive Sponsor 360 Degree Review template that can be used to score candidates against the ART model. 360 Degree Reviews are completed by three or more individuals including the executive sponsor, a peer or superior and the project manager who would lead the project. In areas that show low scoring, an improvement plan should be established to ensure the best possible outcome. This review exercise is a way to narrow down potential sponsors, help identify the most qualified person and set success expectations.

Tools Summary:

- ART Definitions
- Executive Sponsorship 360 Degree Review (Template Found in Appendix C)
- Improvement Plan for Selected Executive Sponsor

Step 3 – Create the Business Case Evaluation (BCE) Document

It is important to identify the potential benefits of strategic initiatives to justify the investment of time and resources to team members and other stakeholders. Most organizations have a business case process that can be used as-is or modified to meet the needs of the project. There are also a variety of good templates that can be found on the internet to suit most needs. As discussed in Chapters 2 and 6, benefits tracking is an important task, and capturing and monetizing these throughout the project is a way to support the original BCE estimates. Together, the executive sponsor and project manager should complete the BCE.

This step also requires the executive sponsor to scan the organization's other, and possibly competing, corporate initiatives to ensure that timing is appropriate for staff resource availability. As an example of the need, one large electric utility required many of the same staff resources for two corporate initiatives that had similar timing. The result was that after nine months, one of the initiatives had to be cancelled resulting in wasted staff time, negative ROI and reflected a poor image on the executive team.

Tools Summary:

- BCE Documentation
- Comparison to Other Corporate Initiatives to Avoid Staff Resource Shortages

Step 4 – Select Team & Execute the Project

As discussed in Chapters 5, 7 and 8 (and related Appendices D, E, F and G), team-based implementation leverages the use of team chartering and project execution tips including a communications plan, meeting agenda/minutes formats, an execution readiness (to launch) review checklist and an execution success status (how is it going) review checklist. These sections should be reviewed to understand the links. Finally, Chapter 8 provides some insight on "getting started" including critical issues and resolution strategies.

This step also requires a constant review of progress and a formal plan-do-check-act (PDCA) cycle for longer, more complex initiatives. Plus, it should include a feedback loop to the original BCE to ensure that the focus has not changed, and the base assumptions are still valid.

Tools Summary:

- Team Charters (Templates Found in Appendix D)
- Communications Plan (Sample Found in Chapter 6)
- Meeting Agenda/Minutes (Templates Found in Appendix E)
- Execution Readiness Survey (Template Found in Appendix F)
- Execution Success Status Review (Template Found in Appendix G)
- Plan-Do-Check-Act (PDCA) Framework with Validation Back to the Original BCE

Step 5 – Team/Project Wrap-Up

This step is usually overlooked but remains an important one in the 5-Step Success model. This is a formal way to review and document lessons learned, what worked/did not work, follow-up on unanticipated outcomes and actions on any future projects or ideas that were identified.

In addition to basic project management tasks, there is a need to celebrate success with the team members. Usually the work is in addition to team members' normal workload, creating extra hours to complete new initiatives. Plus, there are normally "growing pains" along the way from working with cross-functional teams, including their often unique and different cultures. Take time to recognize and reward the team along the way at important milestones, but most importantly, at the project's completion. Communication of the project results is also important and can be done in a variety of ways. One large utility held a free cookout and an awards ceremony at the completion of their project. Another manufacturing team held a group forum with executives and team members to showcase their results, take group photos and published an article in their internal newsletter.

Tools Summary:

- Lessons Learned Meetings (Templates Found in Appendix E)
- Initiate Follow-Up Projects and/or Ideas
- Recognize and Reward Team Members
- Communicate Results (Methods Found in Chapter 6)

It has been said that "collaborative culture change" starts within this 5-Step Success model and the use of cross-functional team engagement.

The ART of Executive Sponsorship™ Lifecycle View

Another way to view the key activities is through an expanded lifecycle view of the 5-Step Process model. As shown in Figure 4-4, the Executive Sponsorship Success Lifecycle incorporates input drivers (called Success Desires) and output processes/tools (called Success Outcomes). The intent of this graphic is to help sponsors understand the "day in the life of an executive sponsor" from inputs and weekly/monthly activities to tools that can be deployed to ensure better positioning for timely completion and a return on investment.

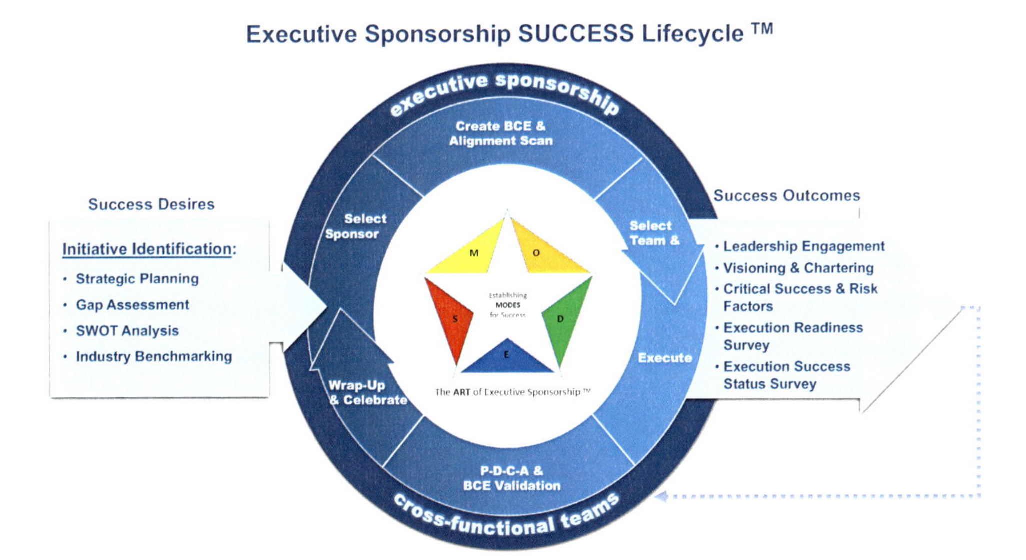

Figure 4-4: The Executive Sponsorship Success Lifecycle

Chapter 5
Team-Based Implementation

As described in Chapters 3 and 4, the strategic planning process includes development of a detailed work plan supported by an executive sponsor. This person serves an important role that should not be overlooked. The individual chosen should hold an executive-level position, have the ability to influence change across functional groups (peers) and be held accountable for delivering desired initiative outcomes. The personal values of this person also are extremely important as he or she will be required to lead by example. Chapter 4 provides a robust framework to help select and provide guidance to assist the executive sponsor through implementation success.

What does "lead by example" mean? It means "walk the talk," be visible, ask "how can I help," and build bridges across departments and groups, which is inevitable in strategic initiatives. An approach used successfully in many cases by initiative sponsors is a team-based implementation model led by a steering team or committee where the overall strategic plan is shared by a group of key stakeholders. Together, they come to agreement on the mission, vision and overall plan. And from these committed parties, others are eventually brought in to help assist in the development and execution of project tasks and related activities. The team-based implementation model should be leveraged when comprehensive strategic initiatives include multiple departments. In this case, cross-functional task teams should be engaged to solve these more complex changes. As shown in Figure 5-1, team members are assigned from various parts of the organizational hierarchy to work in a team-based implementation model reporting to a steering team. For these teams, volunteers should be solicited. Each task team should be established with a formal charter that includes objective, leadership sponsor(s), team individuals (and backups), a list of

Figure 5-1: Team-Based Implementation Model

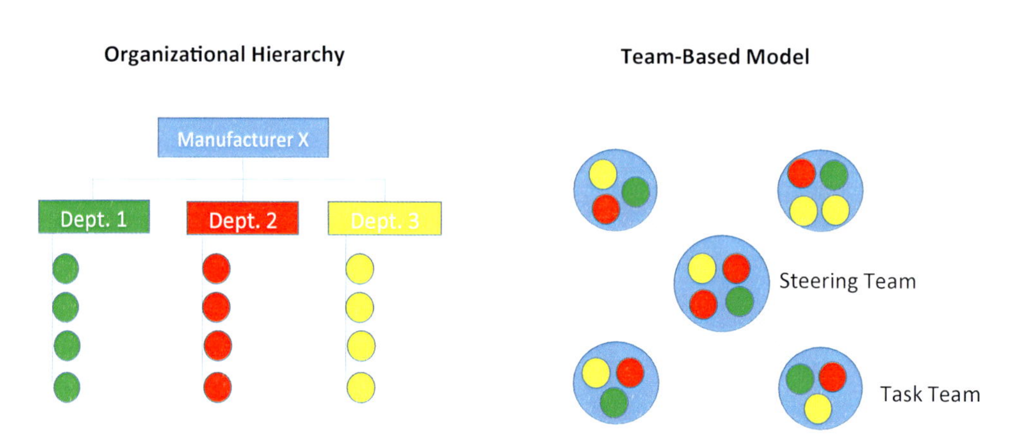

activities with completion schedules and anticipated benefit statements. See Appendix C for example task and steering team charters. Task teams may sometimes separate activities into smaller work groups or sub-teams for a more timely completion schedule. Teams typically create new processes, update or add technology that may require organizational changes and develop documentation and training on new procedures. In some cases, these work teams may need outside training or exposure to peer groups on industry best practices. Therefore, a budget should be established to ensure these activities can be executed. In many cases, outside expertise is brought in to train internal staff on best practices, so the strategic plan also should include a knowledge transfer plan so changes can more readily become embedded and sustainable in the organization.

The steering team should be governed by its own charter, a commitment to each other pledging support, and delivery of initiative execution. The charter should be signed by each member and displayed in a common area frequented by project team members. Some organizations create a "war room" or a dedicated meeting space where initiative team members can hold frequent meetings and display important and often referenced materials on walls, etc.

Once the strategic direction has been established and a detailed work plan and schedule developed, it is important to also review the ability of existing staff to support the initiative and related team efforts. At one large electrical utility company, an asset management strategic initiative failed to get established because key staff stakeholders were already very busy with their normal workloads and supporting a new computerized maintenance management system (CMMS) implementation project.

Figure 5-2: Team-Based Organizational Structure

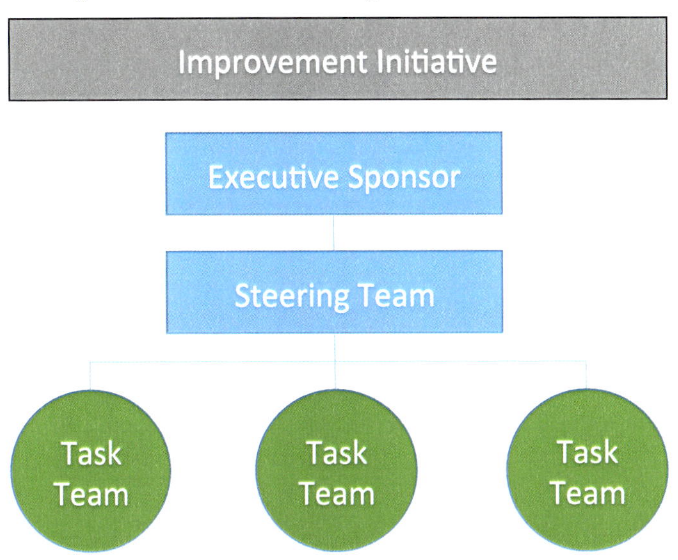

Task Team Organization

- Sponsor (from Steering Team)
- Leader
- Facilitator
- Scribe
- Cross-functional membership

The plan should include a review of staff capabilities and time availability, as well as the potential need for outside support to supplement teams to provide technical expertise, if they do not exist within the organization. The plan should be as detailed as possible and include estimated weekly, monthly and hourly commitments for the sponsor and team members. A simple approach would be to start with estimating the number of teams and team meetings, including follow-up activities. Drafting charters could be one way to create some preliminary time requirement estimates.

Team-based implementation is not a new concept, but there are benefits and some important elements to define, such as team members' roles and responsibilities as listed later in this chapter and shown in Figure 5-2. One benefit of this is knowledge transfer. During a task team presentation to the steering team at a large industrial facility, for example, when asked about experiences serving on the team, a team member stated: "I have learned

Figure 5-3: Example Maintenance Best Practices Initiative Organizational Structure

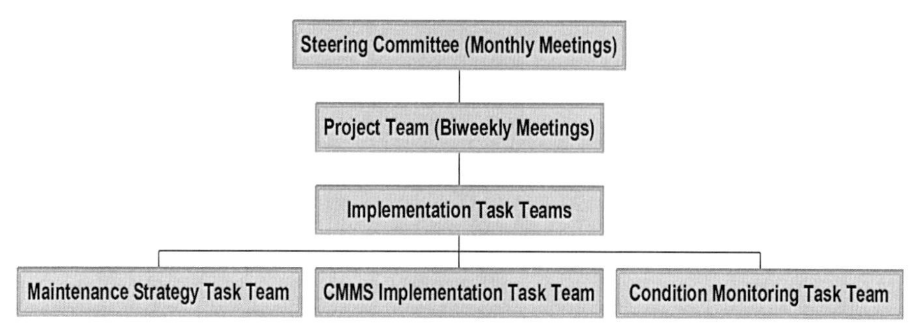

more about our organization in six months on this project team than I have learned in the six years being employed here."

An example of a maintenance best practices initiative at a large utility company is presented in Figure 5-3. It is a good practice to ask for volunteers to make up each team, but in some cases, members may need to be "voluntold" by an appropriate manager or supervisor to get the team initially started. Some organizations like to use a personality trait test to form a rounded mix of team membership, but this may be difficult depending on the size of your organization and available resources.

For a team to be highly effective, there needs to be a solid structure for success. In addition to a formal charter, each team should have these roles and respective responsibilities identified.

Task Team Sponsor

- A representative from the steering team is responsible for overall success of each task team
- Ensures resource allocation (e.g., funding, staff availability, outside support)
- Provides direction and assures accountability
- Responsible for task team outcomes and deliverables, as well as quality and timeliness
- Assists in conflict resolution
- Responsible for team member changes (e.g., removals and additions)
- Mentors and coaches task team leaders
- Coordinates recognition and celebration of success of teams' work efforts
- Assigns a co-sponsor, retains overall responsibility
- Updates corporate executive sponsor and managers on team progress on a regular basis

Team Leader

- Serves as a project manager in delivery of task teams' work
- Assures necessary team training
- Assures effective meeting management
- Serves as a change agent
- Ensures team adheres to values and meeting conduct
- Reports regularly to team sponsor
- Mentors and coaches team members
- Facilitates conflict resolution
- Exhibits model behavior, becoming a leader the team wants to follow

Team Facilitator

- Arranges and assures invitees, facility, materials and equipment
- Prepares and distributes agenda and supporting materials
- Assures effective meeting management

Team Scribe

- Prepares accurate and concise minutes of the meeting and notes and distributes them once they are reviewed by the facilitator and/or another individual

Each meeting should have a formal meeting agenda, followed by meeting minutes within two business days of the meeting. Minutes should clearly identify follow-up tasks to be done in-between meetings, with the name of the person responsible listed by each task and a target completion date. Appendix E provides sample meeting agenda and minutes formats.

Each team is usually engaged to solve a particular problem or establish a new best practice. If a process is modified or a new process developed, new procedures and an accompanying technology tool training plan are required and should be listed on that particular team's charter of activities. At the very least, a follow-up step should be added to assign the task to the appropriate department (e.g., training, technology). This will help ensure sustainment of the newly adopted process. For example, at one organization, a New Procedures Task Team was created with the sole responsibility of updating and training staff members on the new procedures created as part of an asset mangagement improvement program.

Chapter 6
Tracking Progress and Benefits

Chapter 5 identified the use of team-based implementation as a preferred method by many organizations to achieve successful and sustainable change. A key ingredient to this is the use of basic project management tools, such as meeting agendas and meeting minutes. Leveraging this approach is a simple way to help track and monitor implementation progress and document benefits, also known as "wins." As initiative scope and team charter activities are completed, there needs to be a cadence of documentation with an even greater focus on documentation and quantification of financial and non-financial benefits. Capturing and reporting the good news, and sometimes even the bad news, are critical components to change. If there is a problem blocking positive advancement toward a goal, it should be presented to the team sponsor, and if needed, escalated to the executive sponsor, who are there to help remove roadblocks. There also needs to be a regimented process and a designated process owner who is actively looking for, documenting and communicating progress and benefit stories. Be prepared to calculate return on investment (ROI) summaries for individual tasks and activities. Collectively, these will be used by the executive sponsor to validate or update the original business case evaluation (BCE) that justified the project's investment.

One large utility organization categorized savings in two ways: green dollars and blue dollars. Green dollars were actual quantifiable financial savings and blue dollars were estimated savings. An example of blue dollars are estimated cost avoidance savings from a predictive maintenance (PdM) program that captured a pending failure before it occurred. Hence, an actual savings. This organization captured and publicized the PdM program cost avoidance savings as regular communications to the whole organization in a report called, "Find of the Week." In a one-year period, these savings showed a positive ROI for the investment in the PdM program's tools and training. Appendix G includes the Execution Success Status Review tool that can be used during the project execution phase to help leadership teams understand their progress against established success measures.

Another large heavy industrial company established a metrics task team to help identify the most appropriate maintenance measures so improvements could be tracked and communicated on a regular basis. The team completed industry research and provided a recommended short list to the steering team. Once approved, the metrics task team established data quality requirements, processes, technology requirements and training to begin measuring improved performance. The team used a beta testing period before officially launching the new measures and related communications. This company's improvement program was quite extensive and included a variety of other improvement task teams, such as CMMS, warehouse, condition monitoring and preventive maintenance optimization. The team invited key stakeholders to participate in a quarterly forum event to share progress

Figure 6-1: Communications Plan Stakeholder Groups

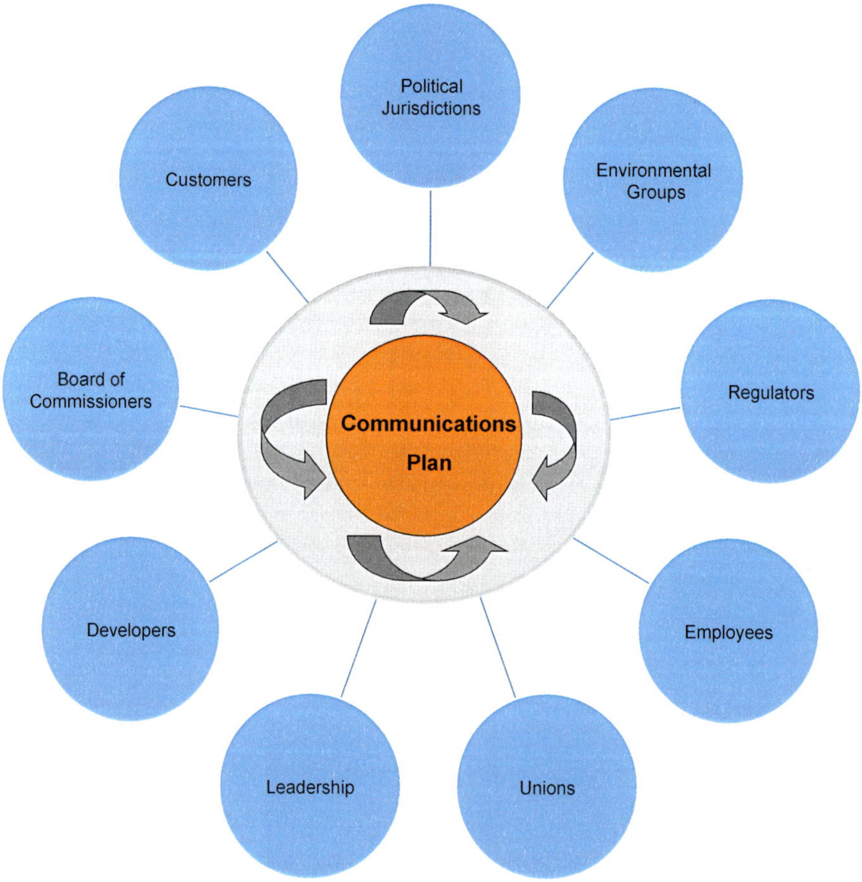

and benefits. This event helped to build staff enthusiasm and project momentum, which led to award-winning status!

Successful organizations have developed formal communications plans and strategies to help create such regimens. As shown in Figure 6-1, it is important that there are methods identified to reach all key internal and external stakeholder groups. Proactive communications tools include meetings, toolbox talks, town hall forums, company newsletter articles, all-staff memorandums and e-mails. Static communications tools include the use of internal websites for team collaboration, intranet sites and document control systems. The focus should be on proactive communications techniques and for them to be most effective, they should be posted on an annual calendar to ensure successful execution. Some organizations have created project logos or graphics to help explain elements and linkages within comprehensive initiatives. As detailed in the Appendix A case study, the project team used a wheel and associated components to explain all the project components as follows.

Figure 6-2: FAMP Wheel

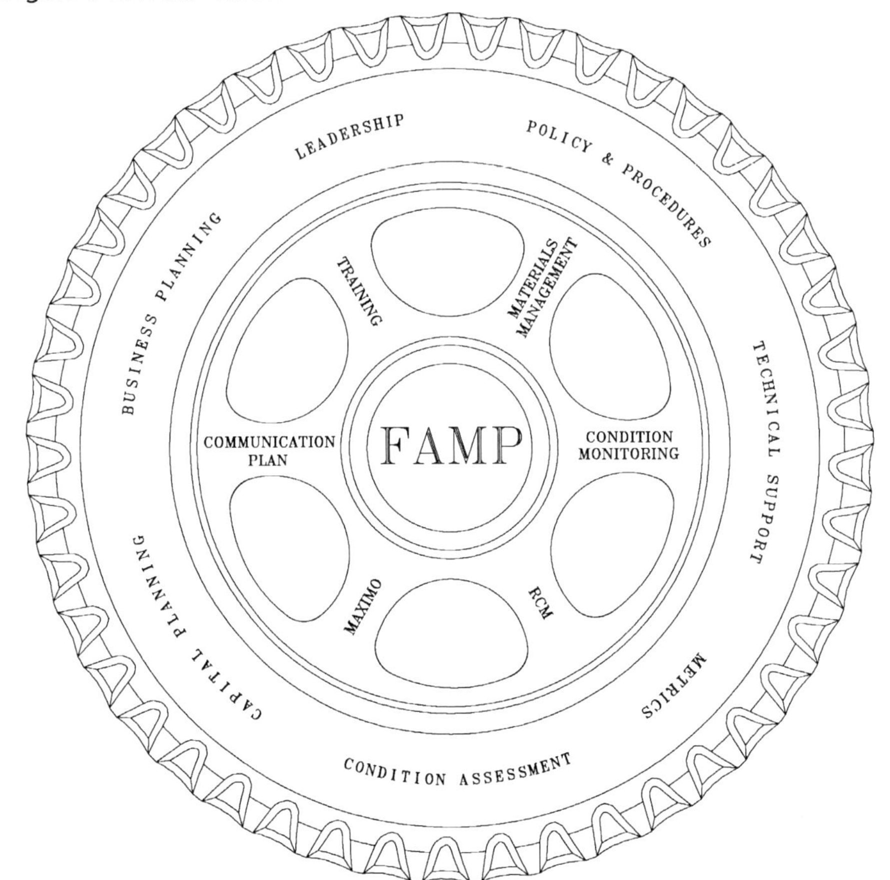

"The wheel model was selected to identify the interrelationship of business practices. The wheel concept was initially conceived to support the development of an intranet site, as well as to clarify confusion between program terminology, such as the facilities asset management program (FAMP) and reliability-centered maintenance (RCM). The wheel concept offers the following: a) Spokes: There are several key components that serve as program supports. If one is missing, the wheel will still turn, but it will be unstable; b) Tire: Many business practices fit into the tire and are integral to the asset management process. If one or several are not in place (low on air), the wheel will still turn, but inefficiently; c) Air Pump: Signifies continuous improvement through research and benchmarking. On occasion, air is lost in the wheel and the air pump is there to maintain proper pressure, allowing peak operating performance; d) Oil Can: As indicated, for the program to move ahead with ease, a master plan/schedule is used to set goals, objectives and milestones. Without such a plan, a program can get bogged down and be ineffective; and e) Tacks: As with any initiative, there are always obstacles/challenges to overcome."

There are four components to an effective communications plan framework that include: the target audiences (who), the messaging (what), the methods (how), and the schedule (when). Here are samples that represent the "Who, What, How and When" of a typical plan.

Target Audiences (WHO)

1) Employees
2) Leadership
3) Stakeholders
4) Regulators
5) Customers

Messages (WHAT)

To effectively communicate the benefits of asset and reliability management, it is important to repeat consistent messages and images (e.g., using as a checklist when preparing the "How").

Key Messages:

Internal

- Asset and reliability management represents the future direction for the company.
- Asset and reliability management includes *all* employees.
- Asset and reliability management leads to better use of limited resources.

- There is a leadership team authorized and expected to implement and communicate the strategic asset and reliability management initiative with a plan, schedule and performance measures.
- Leadership and employees must understand basic principles of asset management and apply them in their daily work.
- Align organizational business processes and decision-making.
- The success of the organization requires the active engagement, collaboration and empowerment of all employees.
- Quality of data matters, and is the foundation for asset and reliability management decisions.
- Supervisors must actively participate in and communicate the strategic asset and reliability management initiative.
- Asset and reliability management is not more work; it's effective, efficient work and actually FREE!
- Leadership will provide appropriate tools and training to ensure success.

External

- Asset and reliability management is a business philosophy that maximizes the use of customer dollars to provide safe and reliable services.
- Our company is proactively addressing safety, environmental issues, aging infrastructure, service to our customers and community sustainability.
- Our company is engaging stakeholders and the public in helping to understand and balance levels of service, cost and protection of our assets and the environment.

Communications Methods (HOW and WHEN)

Table 6-1 depicts an example of communications methods supporting an asset management and reliability initiative.

Table 6-1: Methods of Communications

Communications Type	Purpose/ Description	Target Audience/ Participation	Distribution Channel	Frequency (WHEN)
Presentation	Introduction to asset management and reliability	All employees	Open forum	Once at the meeting, then by e-mail
Fliers on asset management and reliability	Introduction and updates to the asset management and reliability program	All employees	Department meetings and payroll distribution	Once a month
Employee objectives and action plans	Link goals of asset management with employee objectives and actions	All employees, specifically linked to asset management and reliability	Employee performance reviews and individual meetings	Performance reviews
Group presentations	Expand on asset management and reliability definition and progress	All employees	Meetings with leadership	Quarterly
Asset management and reliability supplementary material	Supplement asset management and reliability messages presented in other channels	All employees, stakeholders, some public	Posters, fliers, plans, business documents	Ongoing
Articles and news releases	Reinforce asset management and reliability messages	Employees, elected officials, stakeholders, public	Newsletter, press releases	Quarterly
Intranet	Asset management and reliability updates	Employees	Intranet	Ongoing
Internet	Asset management and reliability updates and base information	Employees, stakeholders	Internet, company website	Ongoing
Advocates	Asset management and reliability updates and reinforcement messages, links to everyday actions	Employees	Training and presentations	As needed
Business plan articles	Asset management and reliability messages, updates, links to the organizational goals	Elected officials, governmental agencies, employees	Business plan	Yearly
Publish	Success stories	National	Trade journals and industry events	Yearly

Chapter 7

Execution Imperatives: The Critical Success Factors

As introduced in Chapter 2 and repeated here as Figure 7-1, FORCE stands for the execution imperatives that can be referred to as critical success factors to help accelerate execution of the strategic plan. In the whirlwind of day-to-day job requirements, it is very difficult to follow-through on commitments made at initiative team meetings. As noted in Chapter 5, the use of formal meeting minutes is a very simple and effective way to track and manage to-do items. One important concept to help ensure the program, project, or initiative is completed is to simply think of it as a capital project. How do you effectively build buildings? How has safety become a culture? If you think of each of these as a capital project, then you can succeed. Key ingredients are a scope,

Figure 7-1: FORCE Strategic Plan Execution Imperatives

Follow-through on activities
Timely
Organized – treat like a capital project
Project Manager
Budget
Respect among team members
Open
Honest
Free Speech
Culture Awareness
Inter Departmental
Culture Awareness
Bottom Up & Top Down
Entrepreneurial
Engaged
Involved
Innovation
Pilot Tests

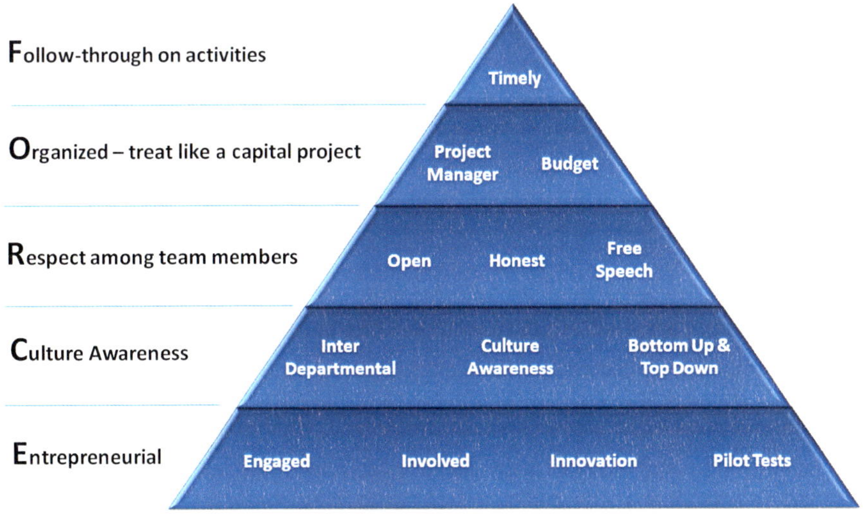

schedule, budget, dedicated project manager and a delivery team. For your strategic plan, assign a dedicated project manager who owns the process from start to finish. *Nothing else but one hundred percent dedication.* In selecting this person, be sure to look for important personality attributes, such as being organized, proactive, flexible, a good communicator and strong facilitation skills, to name a few. Typical strategic plans and change initiatives can take up to a few years, so be sure there is a dedicated budget allocated. Change can happen without financial support and backing, but it will take more time and be seen as the "flavor of the month," and eventually fail.

With the adoption of the team-based implementation approach discussed in Chapter 5, there needs to be a deliberate focus on respectfulness, culture awareness and a zeal for entrepreneurial input. Teams should be diverse with an interdepartmental spread. Asset and reliability management does not solely sit in the maintenance department. If you simply looked at the lifecycle of an asset, you would quickly list departments, such as procurement, engineering, construction, operations, maintenance, finance and information technology. The executive sponsor and steering team are critical in this area. Leveraging the communications plan and ongoing outreach to key stakeholder groups is an important effort to maintain a pulse on the cultural impacts that occur with change and among teams. No team is perfect and there may be times when team members need to be replaced to ensure healthy collaboration.

Early on, initiative leadership should focus on aligning team requirements with individual members' strengths to set them up for success. Mentorship and formal succession planning are two operating principles that can advance and sustain cultural shifts. Understanding individual behaviors and change initiative impacts and outcomes is important and worthy of review to help prepare leadership, shape team membership and direct activities in the communications and work plans. One analysis tool used by successful organizations at the onset of an initiative is a "Strategic Execution Readiness Review" exercise to help document the organization's readiness for change and understand the critical success factors. Appendix F provides a sample readiness survey used by organizations to measure key stakeholders' views on their current state of change readiness. Then, a review of scores can help leadership understand where the plan is strong or weak and allow them to make initial plan adjustments to gain early project momentum. Readiness surveys are also a good tool to measure progress. Simply completing a survey early in the execution schedule and then again six months later can give leadership a sense of improvement. Areas typically covered under a survey include: leadership, vision for change, change strategies, overcoming resistance to change and managing staff performance. Table 7-1 includes a compilation of improvement approaches where scores have been low in certain categories and examples of strategies to help improve scores.

Table 7-1: Example Readiness Improvement Strategies

Readiness Category	Improvement Strategies
1. Leadership	• Establish a Steering Committee • Create a Vision Statement
2. Vision for Change	• Conduct a Gap Assessment • Develop a Communications Plan
3. Change Strategies	• Define Roles / Responsibilities • Review Organizational Needs
4. Overcoming Resistance to Change	• Conduct Feedback / Town Hall Meetings • Apply Team-Based Implementation Model
5. Managing Staff Performance	• Create Skills Training / Development Plans • Update Job Descriptions

Once the strategic plan improvement projects have been initiated, monitoring team progress is an important step. As provided in Appendix G, there is a tool for helping steering teams understand task team progress against established critical success factors. The Execution Success Status Review tool can be scored monthly by steering team members to understand where they are weak or strong in areas they define as critical success measures. A suggested list is as follows:

- Communications
- Benefits Tracking
- Project Management
- Team Chartering
- Leading Change
- Training

The tool can be converted into an electronic spreadsheet format allowing scores to be graphically viewed. Grading can be established for scoring each measure. An example 5-point system follows:

1) Unacceptable
2) Poor, needs improvement
3) Average, but not good enough for us
4) Better than average, but could be improved
5) Exceptional

Figure 7-2: iDEA Model for Maximizing Team Contribution

The **i**DEA Model

Individual Input
Discuss
Evaluate
Act

While it is important to have a good project work plan and schedule, it is also important to use them as a guideline only, allowing for flexibility, individual engagement and innovation. "Involvement breeds commitment" is a quote used by a senior manager during a large change initiative. It has proven to be a true statement when it comes to meaningful engagement from people in the change effort. Steering and other team leaders need to foster a sense of individual entrepreneurship in solving complex problems. And the plan needs to include the time and budget to celebrate successes and wins in order to establish and build momentum and a strong sense of teamwork. At one industrial plant, project workshops would end with a PLUS-DELTA round of feedback, with participants asking each other to identify things they liked or could be improved upon in the future for a more effective meeting outcome. This process allows for continuous improvement and is an opportunity to give praise to those who may have provided good engagement or successfully completed a task. Consider adopting the "no idea is a bad one" concept. This is an area where respect will need to be enforced to ensure open and individual input. As shown in Figure 7-2, the iDEA model is a simple tool that enables leadership and team members to maximize each team member's contribution by following a simple four-step process: **I**ndividual input requested – **D**iscuss as a group – **E**valuate alternatives – **A**ct on the solution. Managers have used this and similar tools to ensure maximum team member engagement to help improve early buy-in and a more timely implementation.

Another proven method to validate and test new ideas and approaches is the use of pilot testing concepts prior to full-scale rollout. One large industrial company wanted to add reliability-centered maintenance (RCM) as a core element of its maintenance best practices program. So, the company selected a process area within the plant to conduct studies using a robust RCM methodology. Upon review of the pilot's results and seeing the enthusiasm from maintenance team members, the company added RCM as a critical element to its program. The company went on to conduct over sixty analyses, which have helped in improving reliability, availability and teamwork between operations and maintenance (O&M) teams and management.

Finally, senior leadership needs to proactively manage workload spread so the typical go-to staff is not overburdened. This approach helps to ensure timelier project completion, cultural alignment and sustainment of change initiatives. In addition, the process of sharing the workload helps to identify otherwise quiet and reserved staff members who could be future leaders. At the company previously noted, a young operator found the RCM program of interest and volunteered to be trained and certified as an RCM facilitator. After successfully conducting several analyses and showing constant improvement, the operator was promoted to a planner/scheduler and then to a maintenance supervisor. Along with advancements, this individual brought along new tools and helped cross-train other O&M staff on best maintenance practices. Today, this same person is in line for a senior asset manager position.

Chapter 8
Getting Started and Sustainment

Some standard questions organizations have when planning to embark on an asset performance or reliability initiative are: How do we get started? What critical issues and pitfalls do we avoid? How do we make this stuff stick? This chapter provides a list of tips and tricks for getting started, speed to implementation and successful sustainment of new processes, tools and approaches. The list is based on experiences with organizations of all shapes and sizes implementing such initiatives.

Getting started typically begins with an executive sponsor who has been handed a problem, opportunity or something more complex, often referred to as "a burning platform." This presents a driver for change. While this is the first step and typically involves a significant investment in resources, there needs to be a clear focus and methodology to ensure successful execution. As noted in the Introduction, it should be clearly understood that there is no "silver bullet" solution nor a straight line trajectory to completion. The world is constantly changing and there likely will be course corrections needed along the implementation phase. Be prepared to accept and adapt to these dynamics and shifts because they will occur! DELTA FORCE is a simple model that has helped many organizations through successful implementation, sustainment of new practices and delivery of ROI.

Prior to embarking on an important initiative, it is recommended that key stakeholders consider the following list of "getting started" points.

1. Identify the Initiative's Executive Sponsor. Attributes to consider:
    - Understands the initiative and future benefits and can articulate those in an "elevator speech"
    - Understands and can help move through potential implementation
    - Ability to solicit team support
    - Ability to articulate the business case evaluation (BCE) for the initiative, and sell resultant benefits to other staff at all levels

- Is committed to the initiative and makes it a TOP priority
- Willing to attend all meetings and author status reports, memos and e-mails
- Is open to obtaining some level of technical training, as required, to understand the technical aspects to improve his or her ability to communicate at all levels
- See Chapter 4 for more details on the attributes, roles and top modes of success (ART) of executive sponsorship.

2. Develop a Strategic Plan
   - Conduct key stakeholder workshops to develop the plan's mission, vision and related documents
   - Conduct key stakeholder workshops to perform a formal review of the problems and/or opportunities (i.e., gap assessment), including the development of an improvement plan and road map
   - Key stakeholders should come from across the organization and at various levels of staff to help them understand that change is coming. Here is where the buy-in to change begins.
   - Identify steering team members and other task teams needed
   - Charter the steering team to own the execution of the improvement plan
   - Review other organizational initiatives, their timing and competing resource needs
   - Consider performing a SWOT analysis in executing the change initiative.

3. Develop Communications and Project Management Plans
   - Identify a full-time project manager
   - Identify a person or team to develop and execute a formal communications plan
   - Identify key performance measures, both (leading and lagging,) to monitor and communicate progress
   - Identify regular/standing meeting schedules (e.g., weekly or biweekly)
   - Adopt formal meeting management templates (e.g., agenda and minutes)
   - Plan for quarterly quality review and plan adjustment check-in dates

4. Identify Team Members
   - Identify task team membership
   - Identify skills requirements
   - Identify need for outside resources (e.g., technical experts, consultants)

5. Select "War Room"
   - Identify room for initiative meetings where key documents (e.g., team charters, project schedules) can be displayed on walls

Table 8-1 shows a list of critical issues to consider, along with example resolution strategies that have been successfully applied on implementing comprehensive, organization-wide asset management and reliability programs.

Table 8-1: Critical Issue Resolution Strategies

Critical Issues	Resolution Strategies
1. Ability to engage key staff members who have time constraints due to normal workloads	• Engage staff deeper in the organization • Use cross-functional work teams to share workload • Expand project schedule • Use outside resources
2. Strong project manager	• Identify staff member with complex project and/or program management experience • Treat initiative like a capital project with an assigned PM, scope, schedule and multi-year budget • Look for a candidate with strong communications, coordination and training skills • Choose a candidate with a strong deputy and administration support staff
3. Leadership engagement and commitment	• Leverage the "ART of Executive Sponsorship" framework to identify and provide guidance tools for success • Program steering team charter endorsed by executive sponsor • Monthly progress and issues resolution sessions • Use of performance metrics and ongoing performance reviews
4. Communications and training	• Create a formal communications plan, including an owner and formal training plan • Track and regularly communicate program progress and benefits and regularly compare to the original BCE • Demonstrate value through the use of pilot programs
5. Schedule and competing initiative coordination	• Align project schedule with other significant organizational initiatives • Complete a staffing support analysis to fully understand staff and resource constraints • Conduct monthly coordination meetings
6. Functional (solo) approach to asset management and reliability	• Utilize a team-based approach where steering and work teams include a cross-functional staff makeup • Provide standard training modules • Clarify and document roles and responsibilities across work streams and program tracks • Conduct quarterly work team status and progress reports and presentations
7. Availability of quality data	• Identify data standards and data owners • Develop data quality review protocols • Establish key performance indicators and a formal performance reporting methodology • Consider an asset management specific IT master plan

Appendix A
A Case Study With Execution Excellence Elements in Action

The following case study was co-presented by this book's author at the 2003 Water Environment Federation's Annual Technical Exhibition and Conference (WEFTEC) held in Los Angeles, California.

PIONEERING ASSET MANAGEMENT IN THE WATER QUALITY INDUSTRY – MWRA'S MODEL FOR CHANGE

John W. Fortin, John P. Colbert and Ted Regan
Massachusetts Water Resources Authority
P. O. Box 100 • Deer Island Treatment Plant • Winthrop, MA 02152

INTRODUCTION

The Massachusetts Water Resources Authority (MWRA) is responsible for providing wholesale water and sewerage services, in whole or in part, to sixty-one communities and 2.6 million people. In addition to its operating responsibilities, MWRA is responsible for rehabilitating, repairing and maintaining the regional water and sewerage systems. Since its assumption of ownership and operations of these systems in 1985, MWRA has undertaken an ambitious program of water and wastewater system capital improvements with estimated expenditures for fiscal years 1986 through 2009 of over $7 billion. Under one massive construction effort, the Boston Harbor Project, the MWRA assumed maintenance responsibility of the $3.8 billion Deer Island Treatment Plant (DITP). As the second largest wastewater treatment facility in the nation, it is designed to treat 1.2 billion gallons per day.

In addition, the Agency had embarked on several other large capital projects that would require similar asset care, including a new water filtration plant.

Figure A-1: Deer Island Treatment Plant

Given the significant value and critical nature of the MWRA's assets, maintenance is of paramount importance. In 1996, the Facilities Asset Management Program (FAMP) initiative was created as a comprehensive, agency-wide effort to most efficiently and effectively manage the region's water and sewer infrastructure.

PIONEERING ASSET MANAGEMENT THROUGH BENCHMARKING

Initially, the multi-phased program was focused on standardization of maintenance practices, adoption of best practices and optimization of labor and material resources. To facilitate the Phase I program and obtain expertise in the area of asset management, a consultant was selected to support MWRA staff.

A maintenance and asset lifecycle strategies survey at outside facilities/industries of similar size and complexity was completed to help develop the FAMP initiative. Survey questions ranged from business and maintenance strategy, organizational structure, staffing and computerized maintenance management systems (CMMS) to asset management, procurement and warehousing policies. Although the survey of water/wastewater facilities found "pockets of excellence," none had an overall asset management model to follow. Upon the consultant's recommendation, the team initiated investigations into the private sector. Fortune 500 and 1000 companies and organizations were contacted and relationships developed. Collaboration efforts were initiated at leading industries, including a steel mill in Canada, a manufacturer in Massachusetts and a process plant in Colorado. In addition, several team members attended and subsequently joined a new professional maintenance association, the Society for Maintenance and Reliability Professionals (SMRP).

Research outside the water quality field helped the MWRA team identify asset management best practices and the MWRA's program model (Figure A-2) and schedules were updated. The benchmarking efforts were a critical turning point in the program's success,

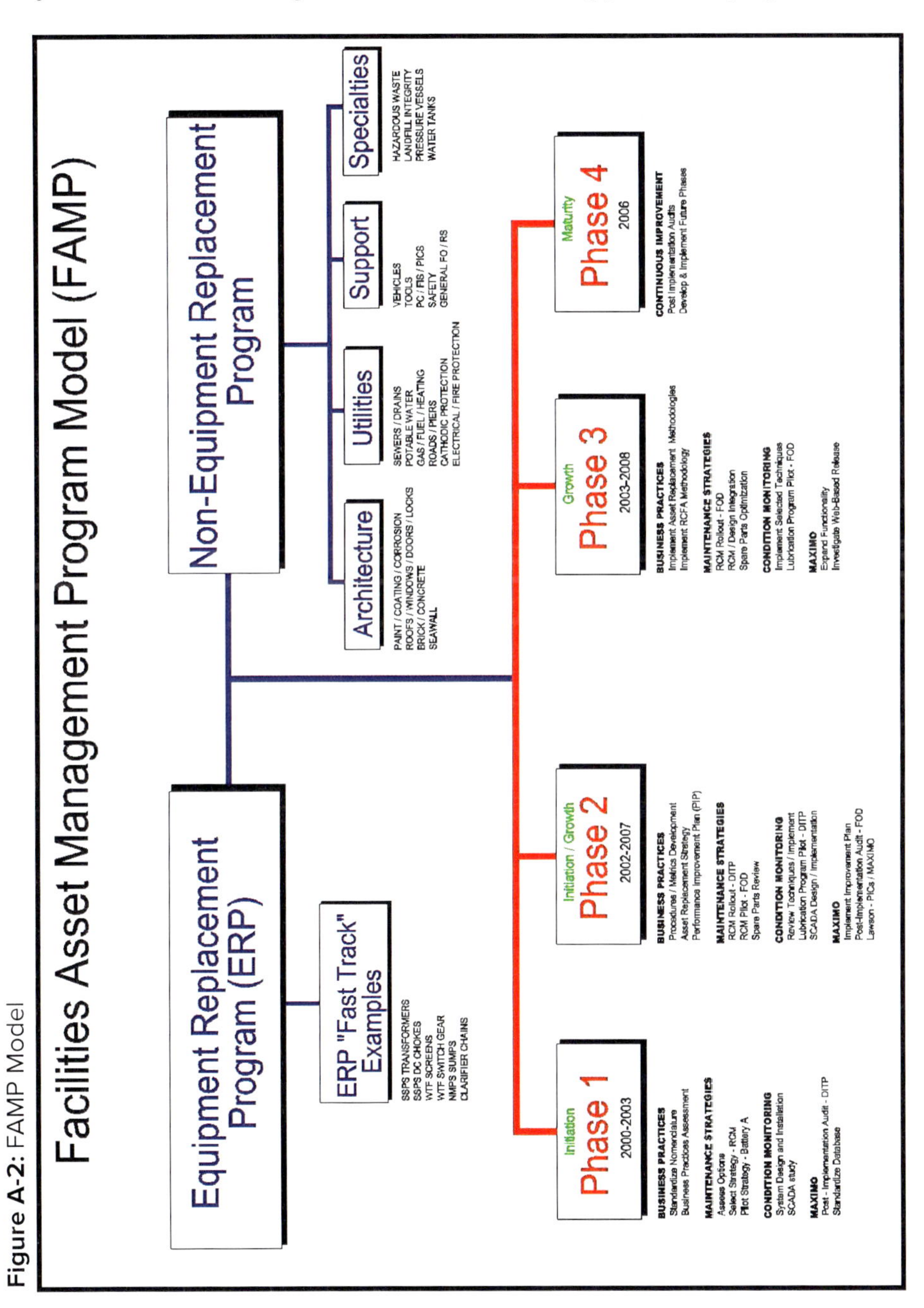

Figure A-2: FAMP Model

allowing the team to identify, understand and incorporate the elements of a comprehensive asset management program.

The MWRA continues to benchmark with other organizations and share their efforts, knowledge and experience with both private and public entities. To date, the MWRA FAMP initiative has received national attention, including:

- The Association of Metropolitan Sewerage Agencies (AMSA) 2002 National Environmental Achievement Award;
- Feature article in the nationally distributed *Maintenance Technology* magazine;
- Host site and case study for MRO Software, Inc., a leading provider of solutions for strategic asset management.

In addition, technical papers and collaborative sessions continue with entities (e.g., associations, public and private organizations), such as the:

- Water Environment Federation (WEF);
- New England Water Environment Association (NEWEA);
- American Water Works Association (AWWA);
- Institute for International Research – Best Maintenance Practices
- General Accounting Office (GAO);
- Society for Maintenance and Reliability Professionals (SMRP);
- Detroit Water and Sewerage Department;
- Seattle's King County Wastewater Treatment Division;
- Gillette Worldwide;
- Coors Brewing Company;
- Intel Corporation;
- Massachusetts General Hospital;
- Massachusetts Institute of Technology (MIT).

The MWRA's benchmarking research and commitment to program implementation has quickly advanced into a recognized benchmark and host site for asset management.

DEFINING ASSET MANAGEMENT

Benchmarking efforts have helped identify key components to a successful asset management program. Asset management is a *formal* and *integrated body of asset lifecycle management practices*. It can be further described as an integrative optimization process that enables a utility to determine how to minimize the total lifecycle cost of owning and operating infrastructure assets while continuously delivering service levels demanded by customers.

The definition of "formal" means that it has been recognized in the organization's business plan and is being treated like a capital project with a manager, budget, scope, schedule and implementation team. "Integrated" means that it touches all business units and applicable processes. "Body of asset lifecycle management practices" means that there are a combination of tools and techniques that, when combined, offer a cost-effective approach to the management of assets throughout their lifecycle (e.g., design, construction, operation, maintenance and renewal).

Benchmarking efforts have allowed the MWRA to redefine its program to include a variety of tools and techniques. The overall objective of asset management is to put an optimal program in place that includes the use of industry best practices. As depicted in the MWRA's FAMP Wheel (Figure A-3), there are many elements to a successful program. However, there are also key components ("spokes"), such as a maintenance strategy (reliability-centered maintenance), a computerized maintenance management system (CMMS), condition

Figure A-3: FAMP Wheel

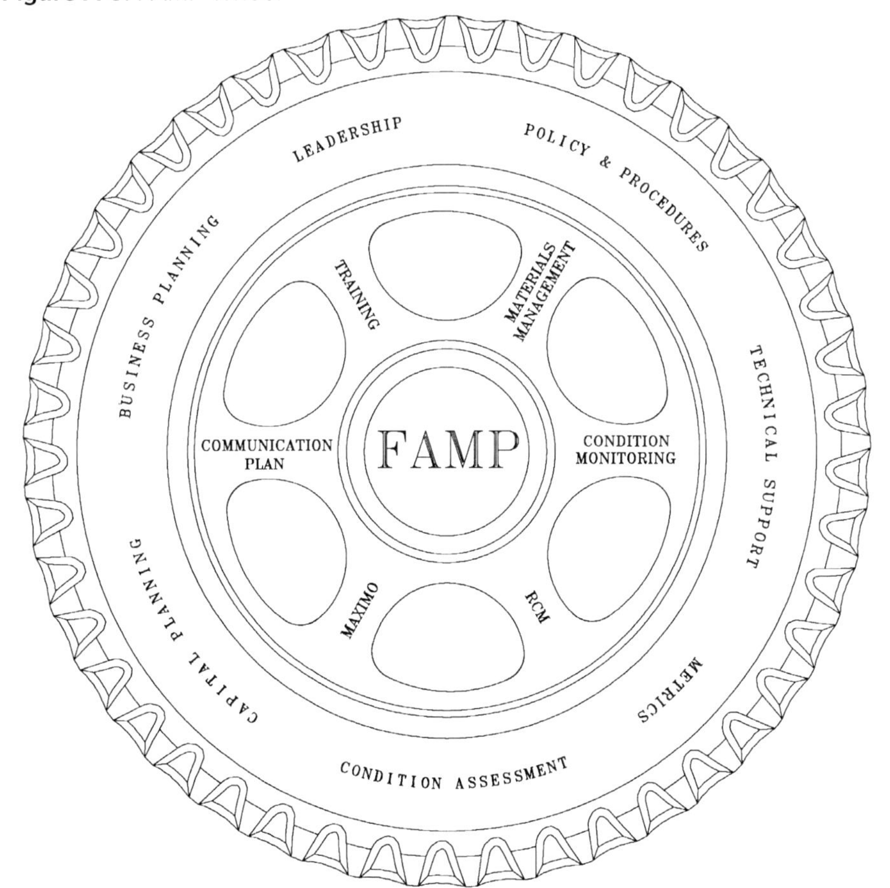

monitoring, materials management, training programs and a regular communications plan. Combined, these elements have led industry leaders to world-class results.

Note that regulations, such as the EPA's Capacity, Management Operation and Maintenance (CMOM) program for the wastewater collection system and the Governmental Accounting Standards Board Statement Number 34 (GASB 34), are only programs that drive ("drivers") utility owners toward asset management. Systems, such as a CMMS and geographic information system (GIS), are only tools that help collect, store and track asset information.

The wheel model was selected to identify the interrelationship of business practices. The wheel concept was initially conceived to support the development of an intranet site, as well as clarify the confusion between program terminology, such as FAMP and reliability-centered maintenance (RCM).

The wheel concept offers these reminders:

- Spokes: There are several key components that serve as program supports. If one is missing, the wheel will still turn, but it will be unstable.
- Tire: Many business practices fit into the tire and are integral to the asset management process. If one or several are not in place (low on air), the wheel will still turn, but inefficiently.
- Air Pump (not shown): Signifies continuous improvement through research and benchmarking. On occasion, air is lost in the wheel and the air pump is there to maintain proper pressure, allowing peak operating performance.
- Oil Can (not shown): As indicated, for the program to move ahead with ease, a master plan/schedule is used to set goals, objectives and milestones. Without such a plan, a program can get bogged down and be ineffective.
- Tacks (not shown): As with any initiative, there are always obstacles/challenges to overcome.

Key Components

Maintenance Strategy: A maintenance plan or strategy needs to be identified for both equipment (active) and non-equipment (passive) assets. For critical equipment assets, the MWRA has selected RCM to define the best preventive and predictive tasks based on the asset's site-specific operating scenario. For second tier assets, the original equipment manufacturer's (OEM's) maintenance recommendations are reviewed and adjusted (optimized), and for support of equipment assets, OEM recommendations are followed.

The non-equipment asset maintenance strategy (e.g., infrastructure, storage tanks, roofs, etc.) includes condition monitoring/assessment and inspection tasks, followed by

Is RCM for All MWRA Assets?

No. It is not appropriate for our non-equipment assets and it wouldn't make sense from a cost/benefit perspective to use it for all our equipment assets. MWRA is applying RCM to only critical/problematic equipment assets (see below), which account for approximately 40% of all equipment.

Equipment	***Maintenance Strategy***
1. Critical/Problematic (e.g., water pumps)	*RCM*
2. 2nd Tier Systems (e.g., DITP hydroturbine)	*PM Optimization*
3. Support Systems (e.g., sump pumps)	*OEM Recommendations*
Non-Equipment	
1. Architecture (e.g., roofs, concrete)	*Condition Monitoring*
2. Utilities	*Condition Monitoring*
3. Support (e.g., vehicles, PCs)	*Condition Monitoring*
4. Specialties (e.g., water tanks, landfill)	*Condition Monitoring*

corrective actions, such as maintenance, small projects, or capital projects. The MWRA's current program is being reviewed, including optimal inspection intervals along with appropriate technique(s) and required skill level.

CMMS: An accurate and maintained computerized maintenance management system is an essential component of a successful asset management program. Maximo®, MWRA's CMMS, is a powerful maintenance management tool that is used to manage all aspects of the maintenance program, including work order management, preventive maintenance, equipment database, planning and scheduling, asset management, recording maintenance costs and generating reports (e.g., monthly and annual maintenance performance reporting).

Condition Monitoring: Monitoring of the equipment's health is an important component of a proactive maintenance program. Condition monitoring techniques, such as vibration, temperature and oil analysis, on rotating machinery are utilized at the MWRA. This non-intrusive approach assists staff in tracking and trending the condition of equipment over time, allowing repair work to be scheduled versus catastrophic failure and associated costs resulting from unplanned reactivity.

Materials Management: Inventory and spare parts play an important role in the asset management program. The challenge is to have the right spares at the right time. Programs are in place to remove obsolete parts, reduce non-critical inventory levels and reduce lead times for materials. There is a strong incentive to reduce inventories to the right levels since there is a twelve percent holding cost for each part.

Training Programs: Training is essential to support the adoption and sustainment of new tools and techniques. For a truly successful program to take hold, it is important to ensure that the staff understands the new programs and their associated benefits. In addition to training on specific applications, such as the CMMS and condition monitoring, training also should be developed for new maintenance work management procedures.

Communications Plan: Early on in the FAMP initiative and as a result of a meeting with another large industrial facility, it was made clear that change management tools would be needed to facilitate change at all levels within the organization. There is a need to communicate that status and results of project activities and their related impact on maintenance business practices. The communications plan is an essential component to a successful maintenance management optimization campaign, allowing connectivity between workforce members and business goals. As expected, the communications plan is a key spoke in the wheel.

MODEL FOR CHANGE

"Leading Change" by John P. Kotter can provide a detailed road map to implement change in an organization through an eight-step change process. Although the MWRA was well along in its program prior to attending an in-house change management course based on Kotter's book, the change process closely mirrored the initiative's development. Therefore, when combined, the eight-step model and MWRA's experience can serve as a framework for successfully implementing an asset management program.

The model for change information is organized as: a) step definition, b) utility opportunities and c) MWRA's experience.

Step 1

Establish a Sense of Urgency – Implementing change at any organization is very difficult. Establishing a sense of urgency to gain support from staff is critical to success. Competitive realities, a potential crisis, or major opportunities can establish a sense of urgency.

The sense of urgency to implement an asset management program at a water quality facility can be driven by the threat of privatization or by mandated federal regulations.

The current economic climate has resulted in a continuing effort by private companies to take over the maintenance and operations of water quality facilities with the promise of reduced rates and better service. The implementation of an asset management program can be a deterrent to privatization by lowering maintenance expenditures through extended asset life, implementation of proactive maintenance approaches that lower costs and communication of proper stewardship of public assets.

A sense of urgency also can come from regulatory "drivers," such as EPA's CMOM programs for buried wastewater infrastructure and GASB's Statement 34 accounting for fixed assets (e.g., asset identification, valuation and remaining service life).

The MWRA was created because wastewater facilities failed prematurely from lack of funding and maintenance (previous control was under the Metropolitan District Commission), resulting in the pollution of Boston Harbor. MWRA's showpiece DITP project, known as the Boston Harbor Project, cost $3.8 billion to construct. The capital expenditures resulted in significant rate increases throughout the MWRA service area. Subsequently, these rate increases drove legislation to study privatization of MWRA's maintenance and operations. The legislation was ultimately defeated, but the threat of privatization remains. The privatization threat and the need to protect new wastewater treatment plant assets established the sense of urgency that led to the creation of an asset management program.

Step 2

Create a Guiding Coalition – A guiding coalition is a group with enough power to lead the change. The group must work together like a team to guide the agency through the change process. The group must work toward a common goal that is pragmatic and can be embraced by the staff.

An asset management steering committee composed of all operations staff could be developed for a water quality organization. The steering committee should meet regularly to discuss the design and implementation of the asset management program. The committee needs to include maintenance, operations, finance, planning and engineering staff. It also needs to include strong upper management support to facilitate and sustain the change process – "*don't tell them, show them.*"

The MWRA formed a steering committee composed of senior managers that continues to meet monthly to discuss the progress and status of the FAMP program. The steering committee is composed of a diverse group of maintenance, operations, engineering, planning and finance staff that represents the various agency divisions. The steering committee's role has been to guide task team efforts and facilitate new maintenance practice implementation.

Step 3

Develop Vision and Strategy – A vision must be created to direct and communicate the change effort. The strategy for achieving the vision must be developed and implemented. The vision is used to clarify the general direction of change, motivate people to take action in the right direction and coordinate the actions of different people in a fast and efficient way.

A utility's vision needs to be documented in the organization's business plan and communicated to all staff. The vision is essential to provide staff with a clear picture of the future. A typical vision for an asset management program could be: "It is our goal to become a leader in the water quality industry for asset management within the next five years. The goal is to reduce maintenance costs through the use of proactive maintenance strategies."

The MWRA Business Plan 2000-2005, the MWRA 5-Year Progress Report 1995-1999 and the FAMP project documents articulated the vision. These documents clearly provided the vision and strategy to initiate and develop a comprehensive program.

Business Plan: The overall MWRA mission statement is: "To provide reliable, cost-effective, high quality water and sewer services that promote public health, promote environmental stewardship, maintain customer confidence and support a prosperous economy." The operations and maintenance goal is to: "Operate the systems safely, within design parameters, and extend the useful life of physical assets." One operations and maintenance objective is to: "Maintain systems to achieve optimum performance." One strategy objective, Strategy #21, is to: "Develop and implement an agency-wide, multi-year maintenance plan." Strategy #21 led to the development of the FAMP request for proposals (outsourced consultant support).

The 5-Year Progress Report: This document states: "Looking ahead, a number of imperatives are presented. MWRA must invest in maintenance and equipment. MWRA must press forward on equally important new expenditures for maintenance and normal replacement and renewal of equipment in its facilities. It would be fiscal folly not to properly maintain the huge investment that ratepayers are making in new water and wastewater infrastructure systems."

The FAMP project bid document states that: "The initiative is designed to plan, manage and coordinate the engineering maintenance, operations and financing required to maintain MWRA's facilities to regulatory requirements. FAMP can be further described as having two objectives:

1. Cost-effectively replace capital components at the appropriate time to ensure reliable plant operation and preserve the value of the original investment.

2. Prolong the equipment life and control the rate of replacement (i.e., avoid large spending spikes)."

Step 4:

Communicate the Change Vision – Every vehicle possible must be used to constantly communicate the new vision and strategies. Guiding coalition members' behavior must serve as the role model for employees.

As a first step, a water quality utility needs to develop a communications plan. The plan should include all elements expected to inform and encourage employees to participate in the program. Elements should include presentations by senior staff to reinforce management's commitment to the program and that it is not the "flavor of the month" program. It is also important that the staff be recognized for program accomplishments. Finally, management must continually communicate the importance of the program.

The MWRA employed various means to communicate the change vision. Table A-1 is a listing of all the activities, including frequency and responsibility, used to communicate FAMP's objectives. As noted, program goals and objectives were communicated through meetings, presentations, posters, hats, awards and daily discussions with the staff. One important first step in the communications plan was Director of Deer Island, John P. Vetere, meeting with all staff to introduce and discuss FAMP's concepts and terminology and openly expressing his support of the program. In addition, triannual forums are held with task teams and other staff to not only communicate program status and benefits, but

Table A-1: MWRA's Communications Plan

METHOD	FREQUENCY	AUDIENCE
RCM Briefings	As needed	DITP – All Staff
RCM II Hats	As needed	RCM Analysis Members
FAMP Project Meetings	Biweekly	FAMP Project Team Members
FAMP Steering Committee Meetings	Monthly	MWRA Senior Management
FAMP Task Team Meetings	As needed	Task Team Members
Board Staff Summaries	As needed	MWRA Board of Directors
RCM 3-Day Training	As needed	MWRA Staff
RCM 1-Day Training	As needed	MWRA Senior Management
Site Visit and FAMP Presentations	As needed	MWRA Staff
FAMP *This Week* Articles	Monthly	All MWRA Staff
All-Staff Status Memorandums	Quarterly	DITP – All Staff
RCM Pilot Project Status Board	Monthly	DITP Staff and Visitors
RCM *Welcome to Pilot* Board	Continuous	DITP Staff and Visitors
Maintenance Performance Report	Monthly	MWRA Senior Management
Reliability Process Model (Poster)	Continuous	DITP – All Staff
RCM Implementation Plan (Poster)	Continuous	DITP – All Staff
Staff Informational Update Meetings	Monthly	DITP Staff
FAMP Intranet Site	Continuous	All MWRA Staff

to drive task team activity to completion. Lastly, an information kit was developed and subsequently converted to an intranet web page that provides details and updates to a wider audience. Communication of the change vision continues daily.

Step 5:

Empowering Broad-Based Action – Broad-based action can only be achieved by removing obstacles, changing systems and structures that undermine the change vision, and encouraging risk-taking and nontraditional ideas and actions.

The steps in broad-based action for a water quality utility could include:

- Reorganize to support the asset management initiative;
- Define areas of improvement that provide the highest return on investment;
- Implement pilot programs to start the change process;
- Benchmarking.

The organizational structure for an asset management program requires a "champion" at the highest level in management. Division champions then need to be assigned at each facility and, finally, staff schedules must allow availability to work on the program.

One method to target areas for improvement is to utilize a consultant to perform a GAP analysis. A GAP analysis is a process where a maintenance consultant reviews your maintenance processes and identifies areas for improvement and weaknesses that can result in long-term maintenance savings. The GAP analysis results are shared with the staff and a corrective action plan (CAP) developed. The CAP could include the use of pilot programs to help provide cost-benefit justifications prior to full implementation.

A second method to determine improvement target areas is to benchmark against other agencies and organizations and to attend conferences dedicated to asset management, such as the Society for Maintenance Reliability Professionals (SMRP). The benchmark effort should be with both water quality agencies that are working on asset management and outside industries that have adopted an asset management approach. Site visits should be attended by staff members responsible for program implementation, thus allowing for a collective agreement and approach to the required improvements.

MWRA Reorganization

The MWRA's reorganization approach created a steering committee to oversee the development and implementation of the program with representatives throughout the agency. Two full-time positions were created to assist in the design, implementation and sustainment of the program. The capital program manager position is responsible for related contract development, oversight and support, including outsourced support, such as con-

Figure A-4: Phase I Organization Structure

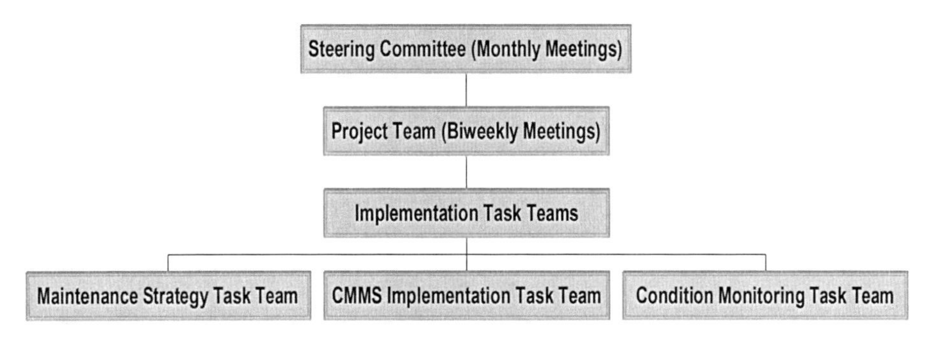

sulting and condition monitoring services. The maintenance asset manager is responsible for program implementation and performance monitoring. The initial focus of these positions was to manage the Phase I maintenance consultant's contract and implement subsequent improvement recommendations. The Phase I scope can be summarized into three categories: maintenance strategy development, CMMS implementation and condition monitoring. To support the consultant's efforts and facilitate staff buy-in, three task teams were formed composed of all levels of staff throughout the agency – "*involvement breeds commitment.*" The Phase I organization chart is shown in Figure A-4.

MWRA Areas Selected for Improvement

Three areas initially selected for improvement were maintenance strategy improvements, CMMS implementation and condition monitoring.

- Maintenance Strategy Review

  The consultant reviewed various maintenance optimization strategies, including reliability-centered maintenance (RCM), total productive maintenance (TPM) and failure modes, effects and criticality analysis (FMECA), for use in the wastewater treatment industry. A detailed report recommended that RCM should be used for the DITP pilot.

  Initiated in the aviation industry, RCM is a process where plant maintenance, operations and engineering staff review failure modes and effects and develop a preventive/predictive maintenance program based on the equipment's operating context. History has shown that the equipment vendor's preventive maintenance (PM) recommendations tend to be conservative and do not always adjust for varying operating scenarios (e.g., does the pump run continuously for twenty-four hours, cycle on-off every forty minutes, or run once a week for ten minutes).

RCM was selected because, historically, its review process was found to be more effective in process plants where the TPM strategy better supports a manufacturing (i.e., close operator to machine interface) environment. Overall, RCM has been able to meet the MWRA's main objective of gaining efficiency of maintenance resources while maintaining or increasing plant reliability.

- CMMS Improvements

  Deer Island has been using Maximo® as its CMMS software since 1995. This software package is a powerful maintenance management tool that is used by the work coordination group to manage all aspects of the Deer Island maintenance program.

  The maintenance consultant completed a post-implementation audit of Deer Island's Maximo® database that included a review of its data quality and its present utilization.

Data Quality

The audit concentrated on one thousand, two hundred and fifty pieces of plant equipment in a section of the plant called Primary Clarifier Battery "A." The review included a three-pronged approach, where data was cross-compared between the Maximo® database (equipment, inventory, preventive maintenance and work orders modules), field nameplate data and technical information (operations and maintenance manuals and process and instrumentation diagrams) located in the on-site technical library. As expected, the audit concluded that the quality of data in Maximo® needed to be improved because equipment was missing from the database, not all equipment data was completed and data conflicted between Maximo,® the field and the library. A corrective action plan (CAP) is underway where thirty percent of the Maximo® data has been corrected, with a target completion date of 2006. To avoid future data quality issues, new procedures (as noted later) have been developed and implemented – "*garbage in is garbage out.*"

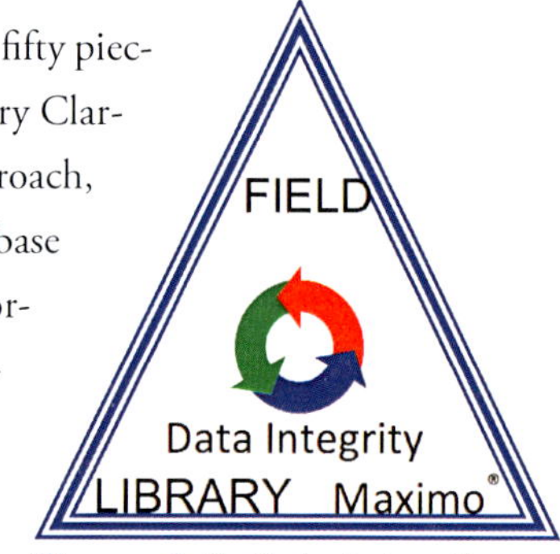

Figure A-5: Data Integrity Triangle

Utilization of the Maximo® system

The review revealed that Deer Island was utilizing approximately two thirds of the available Maximo® features (termed "functionality") which, reportedly, is the case with most other maintenance organizations. To enhance the data quality and support a new asset management initiative, the consultant recommended additional utilization of specific Maximo® modules and programming enhancements, including failure reporting, safety plans and required fields. A corrective action plan (CAP) was developed as a result of the audit and failure reporting and required fields for work orders were completed in 2002.

Other recommendations were made to support the initiative, including: a) programming for performance metrics reporting; b) programming for run time PMs versus calendar-based maintenance, reducing workload/costs; c) Quality assurance and quality control (QA/QC) procedures to protect the Maximo® data used to make business decisions, such as equipment replacement; and d) programming to link Maximo® to the financial software package (Lawson™) to allow automatic tracking of nonstock items and improve the planning process for parts and kitting of materials.

- Condition Monitoring

  The Authority recognized that the project's maintenance optimization process would require expanding predictive maintenance tasks, including vibration and temperature trending and analysis. Phase I included the design and installation of permanent vibration and temperature monitoring on critical rotating equipment, such as pumps, motors, compressors and turbines.

  The new condition monitoring system design has been completed and installation is anticipated to begin in 2003.

MWRA Pilot Implementation

A pilot of the new RCM maintenance strategy was completed under consultant guidance. The RCM pilot consisted of twelve systems from a cross section of equipment located in the Primary Clarifier Battery "A" section of the plant. The pilot system's performance was compared to adjacent equipment, which uses OEM-based PM tasks and frequencies, for a six-month period.

The pilot results included a significant decrease in PM hours, a twenty-five percent reduction in PM labor hours and a ten percent overall decrease in maintenance costs. In addition, the pilot area has resulted in higher equipment availability and overall improved performance. The major outcome of the RCM review process is a revised, optimal mix of predictive and preventive maintenance tasks and frequencies that best meet the plant's operating goals.

Early on in the asset management program's history, the pilot was a major contributor to the organization's cultural change. Commitment to the RCM methodology was significant and over one hundred staff members were involved in the pilot.

Benchmarking

A key component to the change momentum was through research. At various stages of the program, teams of in-house staff collaborated with outside companies and organizations to understand time and cost-saving approaches, views and benefits. The focus was put on other organizations of similar size and complexity. It was quickly determined that advanced knowledge in the area of asset management was limited within the water quality facilities arena, so the need to look at outside entities was required. Collaboration efforts were initiated at leading industries, including a steel mill in Canada, a manufacturer in Massachusetts and a process plant in Colorado. In addition, several team members attended and subsequently joined a new professional maintenance association, the Society for Maintenance and Reliability Professionals (SMRP). SMRP offers an opportunity to gather best practices information from a large network of maintenance and operations professionals at Fortune 500 companies. This research helped team members communicate the benefits of a comprehensive asset management program to all levels of staff through the use of real-life success stories.

Step 6:

Generating Short-Term Wins – To continue to show the importance of the change, it is important to have short-term wins to show employees the success and importance of the change. Wins needs to be planned/created and people visibly recognized and rewarded for making the wins possible. An effort to plan for visible improvement in performance (wins) should be developed.

One method to consider for generating short-term wins is to leverage pilot results to provide opportunities for staff recognition and awards. A second method is to communicate program (i.e., pilot) results and benefits to all employees through presentations, staff meetings, memorandums and posting information in high traffic areas. A third method is to publish articles in professional organizations or recognized trade magazines.

The MWRA generated wins by communicating the results of the RCM pilot and its status, results of other FAMP program implementation efforts and related case study articles in trade magazines, such as *Maintenance Technology* magazine. The benefits included actual cost savings, as well as soft benefits, such as increased staff knowledge and improved operations and maintenance teamwork. To recognize the staff's dedication to the program while balancing normal workloads, the internal "Excellence in Performance" award was presented to all program participants by the executive director and chief operating officer.

In May 2002, the MWRA's FAMP initiative also received national attention at the Association of Metropolitan Sewerage Agencies' (AMSA) 2002 National Environmental Achievement Awards in the *Operations* category. In addition, the program was recognized in a feature article in the nationally distributed *Maintenance Technology* magazine. These short-term wins helped fuel the program's momentum and furthered management and staff support.

Technical papers and presentations detailing the program's successes were also accepted at local, national and international organizations, such as the New England Water Environment Association (NEWEA), the Society for Maintenance and Reliability Professionals (SMRP), the Water Environment Federation (WEF) and the Institute for International Research – Best Maintenance Practices. More importantly, these wins were shared with the staff to communicate the program's success.

Step 7:

Consolidating Gains and Producing More Change – Gains should be used to produce more change. Increased credibility should be used to change all systems, structures and policies that don't fit together or don't fit the transformation vision. People should be hired, promoted and trained to implement the change vision. The process should be reinvigorated with new projects, themes and change agents.

A water quality organization needs to move forward from the pilot programs to a full rollout of the selected initiatives. The rollout of the program requires a greater commitment of staff resources and management support.

Figure A-6: MAPP

The MWRA's approach to consolidate gains and produce more change was to: a) roll out the initiatives developed during Phase I activities and the pilot; and 2) expand the program based on benchmark findings. An expanded multi-phase program model and master asset protection plan (schedule) or MAPP (Figure A-6) were developed, detailing a comprehensive asset management program.

The program was expanded from three to ten task teams to guide the Phase II rollout. Each task team developed a charter with goals and responsibilities to facilitate the implementation of best practices throughout the organization. The task teams have support throughout the Authority and include representatives from maintenance, operations, process control, finance, budgeting, planning, warehouse and management.

The task teams and their charters include:

- **Metrics** – Develop consistent metrics to monitor program implementation and to drive higher plant reliability and availability.

- **RCM Implementation** – Ensure the RCM program is implemented uniformly throughout the Authority including:
    - Monitor and track effectiveness of the RCM program;
    - Develop and monitor organization-wide rollout plan and schedule;
    - Implement RCM recommendations and associated tracking/reporting.
- **Criticality Analysis** – Develop and implement a criticality analysis agency-wide to help prioritize systems for RCM analysis, as well as assist in the prioritization of corrective maintenance (CM) work.
- **Condition Monitoring Program** – Develop and implement a condition monitoring program to further assist the change from reactive maintenance to proactive maintenance. This team's focus is to expand current programs, such as oil analysis and vibration monitoring, into comprehensive programs that provide early indication of failures and prevent costly repairs. A needs assessment and implementation and training plan is underway and involves other areas, including infrared, ultrasonics and motor current signature analysis (MCSA).
- **Permanent Condition Monitoring System Installation** – Oversee the design, installation and testing of permanent vibration and temperature monitoring on critical equipment to provide higher equipment availability and improve maintenance efficiency.
- **Maintenance Procedures** – Develop and implement new practice procedures and training to ensure adoption and change sustainment.
- **Asset Replacement Strategy** – Develop a comprehensive and consistent agency strategy to identify and prioritize asset replacement needs, resulting in more accurate spending forecasts and determination of appropriate funding sources.
- **Warehouse Optimization** – Develop and implement consistent and efficient warehouse activities in an effort to support maintenance, including spare parts analysis, work order kitting, purchasing inventory replenishment, spare parts maintenance policies and obsolescence of identified materials.
- **Work Coordination/Maximo®** – To ensure efficient use of Maximo® to assist in the timely coordination and execution of maintenance and asset replacement planning activities.
- **Lubrication Program** – Improve the handling, storage, sampling, application and purchasing of lubrication products, leading to extended asset life.
- **Root Cause Failure Analysis** – This future team will review and implement the consultant's recommendations associated with a preferred RCFA methodology. A RCFA program focuses on investigating and eliminating chronic problems.

Each task team is led by a staff facilitator who coordinates regular meetings to detail progress and future plans. The task team approach and expanded scope have impacted all areas of the Authority's business and have been effective in the change process.

Step 8:

Anchoring New Approaches in the Culture – As the last step in the eight-step process, the new business practices need to be anchored in the organization's culture. The connections between new behaviors and organizational success need to be articulated. There is a need to create better performance through productivity-oriented behavior, better leadership and more effective management.

A utility can anchor change by conducting presentations and meetings that communicate the culture change and detail the scope of work, progress to date and the benefits of the program. In addition, adoption of leading and lagging performance metrics can be utilized to move the organization to more proactive and productive behavior. These metrics need to be shared with all staff and even posted in common areas, and be frequently reviewed by management.

The MWRA has begun anchoring the new approaches by conducting regular FAMP forums, implementing the productivity improvement program (PIP) and the MAPP, monitoring implementation status and adopting new maintenance metrics.

FAMP forums, attended by the task team members, management and plant staff, are regularly held to discuss the status, progress and benefits of the task teams. The forum provides a global perspective of the entire FAMP program to approximately one hundred staff members over a two- to three-hour session. At each forum, Chief Operating Officer Mike Hornbrook reinforces the commitment of management to the FAMP initiative.

PIP is a multi-year negotiation with two unions in an effort to institute cross-functional job descriptions. The areas concentrated on are cross-functional (mixed) crews and operations staff performing light maintenance duties.

In March 2002, mixed crews were implemented in all plant areas. A mixed crew includes electricians, instrumentation and controls (I&C) technicians, maintenance and operations (M&O) specialists, HVAC technicians and plumbers, all led by a single unit supervisor. The mixed crew format increases efficiency by reducing downtime waiting for specific trades to support a multi-discipline work order. In addition, light maintenance, such as HVAC filter changes, lightbulb replacements and lubrication, are now assigned to an area maintenance team and/or operations, not to a specific trade. In the maintenance group, this has allowed the unit supervisor flexibility to assign these tasks to any one of a number of staff members based on their availability and priorities of the week and day.

A portion of light PM maintenance tasks has been assigned and performed by operations staff, including inspections and lubrication. Metrics are utilized to anchor the new culture, including:

- Tasks performed represent eleven percent of PM hours and fifteen percent of all PMs.
- This represents a fourteen percent increase in work orders assigned to operations staff since the start of PIP implementation in March 2002.
- The best in class goal accepted by the Society for Maintenance and Reliability Professionals is ten to fifteen percent of all PM hours.
- The improved productivity of plant staff has resulted in maintaining plant backlog to within industry guidelines of four to six weeks, with fewer staff and increased plant availability.

The MAPP was developed to establish a long-term schedule for the four elements of the program: Business practices, maintenance strategies, condition monitoring and Maximo®. This schedule is posted in common areas, cementing management's commitment to staff.

On a regular basis, an implementation status report is provided to senior management and includes a compilation of task team activities and status of completion, thus helping to drive task team activity.

Metrics were developed for proactive and productivity initiatives. Annual goals are monitored through monthly metric reporting. Metrics are reviewed by senior staff and are available to staff via the MWRA intranet site.

The proactive metrics included the percentage of preventive maintenance work orders that are kitted and the percentage of predictive maintenance work orders. The kitting metric is driving change for both the work coordination/planning department and the warehouse in an effort to ensure parts are available prior to work initiation. This is resulting in work efficiency in the form of increased wrench time. The planners identify all PM parts in the Maximo® system and the warehouse retrieves the parts each month and places them on pallets for maintenance pick up. The predictive maintenance metric is driving change for the maintenance staff and the condition monitoring group. A goal has been set to increase predictive maintenance tasks. To reach that goal, the condition monitoring group has initiated staff training and increased the oil and vibration sampling programs.

The productivity metric is the percentage of PMs performed by operations. This metric has driven both maintenance and operations to add light maintenance tasks to operations staff as discussed earlier. The use of metrics has been successful in anchoring change.

Challenges – Along with any change initiative, there are challenges along the road to improvement. Initiating any new program has many challenges and obstacles, and asset management is no exception. Trying to design and implement a comprehensive, organization-wide program will have more obstacles because of the magnitude of required change across departmental boundaries. The use of a steering committee, whose body includes broad representation, can lessen the impact. Some reminders to avoid common challenges to implementation are:

- Executive sponsorship and a communication plan are critical to effect culture change.
- Program elements require leaders with a clear charter and diverse membership.
- Funding and resources must be reserved and used to help maintenance during the implementation period. Remember, folks are balancing normal workloads while implementing change.
- Treat the asset management program as a capital project with a budget, dedicated staff, schedule with milestones and involvement from all business functions.
- Do not expect overnight change or results; it is a multi-year implementation project – *"How do you eat an elephant? In small bites!"*
- Staff buy-in is essential. "But we've always done it this way" or "I recommended this, but nobody listened" are some common responses from staff when it comes to implementing change. Learn to let go and invite staff members to become team members and get involved – "*involvement breeds commitment.*"
- Show staff "what's in it for them." For example, understanding that feedback on work orders is to identify repetitious problems and/or poor products. Documented problems can lead to a design change that will eliminate the headache. In the public world of low bid, the documented poor product can be removed from the specification.
- Change agent characteristics include optimism, organization and persistence.
- Individual or team recognition should be posted when goals are met.
- Track and document results and benefits. Communicate these broadly, early and often.
- The CMMS must be populated with accurate data. Poor data results in incorrect and inaccurate work orders and reporting that impacts morale and business decisions. Make sure a budget line item is in place for a post-implementation audit of your system.
- OEM preventive maintenance tasks are guidelines and typically not operation specific. A maintenance optimization review will confirm proper tasks and frequencies to ensure extended asset life and heightened reliability.

- Training, even on new procedures, must be provided to ensure employees feel well prepared for the new program.

GETTING STARTED

A water quality utility can get started with an asset management program with strong senior management support and a few dedicated resources working on the program. One key step is to identify a "management champion" who has enough power to drive the organizational change. Most organizations have some portions of the model of change in progress. Referring to the previously described eight-step process, usually Step 1 is already in place. To get started, Steps 2 through 5 need to be developed.

BENEFITS

It is inherent that there are tremendous benefits associated with the implementation of an asset management program. In addition, there is a tremendous amount of resources and data available to help utilities justify an investment in such a program. Until a utility's program is mature enough to recognize benefits and results, benchmarking and case studies can certainly help.

The MWRA has experienced significant benefits to date, including cost savings, extended asset life, enhanced teamwork, better communications and process efficiencies. Here is a representative sampling.

Maintenance Strategy – RCM

- The DITP RCM pilot demonstrated a twenty-five percent reduction in PM hours by eliminating duplicate work by maintenance and operations staff, and eliminating low value PM work. In some cases, PM hours have increased to provide additional protection for plant assets.
- Extended asset life through a revised operating context. An RCM review revised a headwork's standard operating procedure (SOP) to rotate the grit pod inlet nozzle in quarter turn increments to equalize wear from abrasive grit, thus extending the pod's life by four. There are twelve pods in all.
- Enhanced O&M staff teamwork as a result of the RCM process. Together, O&M staff jointly analyze critical asset operations and failure modes. Each comes away with a greater appreciation of the others knowledge and experience. In addition, the audit process builds bridges between management and O&M staff, where management audits and approves the staff-authored maintenance program.

CMMS

- Cost savings from meter-based PM program. A distributed control system (DCS) to Maximo® interface has been developed to automatically generate work orders based on equipment run hours. The previous approach was calendar-based maintenance that sometimes recommended maintenance on equipment that had limited operating time and did not require maintenance. In two pump stations, only eight out of twelve pumps received PM. If a calendar-based system were in use, four units would have potentially received unnecessary maintenance.
- Utilization of work backlog information to support staffing business decisions. For example, instrumentation backlog is high (greater than the industry average of four to six weeks) and additional staff may be required to maintain these assets.
- Scheduling work one week in advance over a three-month pilot at DITP resulted in reducing work backlog and a twenty-five percent increase in work order completion.
- A program has been written to capture duplicate work requests resulting in efficiencies, such as eliminating duplication of labor efforts and combining multiple work efforts to reduce visits to the same asset.

Condition Monitoring

- Asset life is extended through the adoption of oil sampling and vibration analysis programs that identify potential problems early and are resolved prior to extensive asset damage.
- Cost savings were realized from an oil sampling program versus calendar-based oil changes. Annual oil changes on aerators and mixer gearboxes were revised to a six-month sample of the oil on condition task. The benefit avoided thirty-three unnecessary annual oil changes, resulting in a saving of approximately twenty thousand dollars in synthetic oil purchased and a disposal cost of six hundred and forty gallons of oil in one year.
- Oil analysis results facilitated the replacement of a 480-volt transformer before failure. Electrical distribution system component (bus ducts) failures caused electrical stressing of other system components, specifically 480-volt transformers that service the power plant. The oil sampling program identified an increase in combustible gas in the transformer's oil. Regular testing and trending of the data provided an early failure warning and a need to replace the unit, a unit that requires a fourteen-week lead-time for delivery. Oil condition monitoring allowed timely replacement of a long lead item and prevented a catastrophic failure, potential safety incident and secondary damages and associated costs.

- A wastewater pump shaft bearing had abnormal vibration readings. The bearing was greased and vibration returned to normal vibration levels. Work was completed during a normal work shift. The cost avoidance was a twenty-five thousand dollar bearing replacement and maintained availability of a critical asset.
- The DITP residuals digester gas compressor chiller had high vibration readings. The repair included checking hardware and adding oil prior to returning the unit to service. The actions prevented a failure and the replacement of a ten thousand dollar compressor.
- Staff morale has increased from involvement in activities, such as the lubrication task team. Team members are allowed to develop and implement a comprehensive program based on their research.

Materials Management

- Kitting ensures spare parts are available prior to work initiation, resulting in work efficiency.
- A spare parts prioritization process has been developed and implemented, leading to the identification of critical spares and cost savings from reduced spares inventory.
- A spare parts preventive maintenance program has been expanded to adequately maintain spare parts held in inventory. Proper maintenance of spares eliminates premature failure (i.e., "infant mortality") upon use.

Training

- Increased staff morale from involvement in condition monitoring equipment training. Training on new ultrasonic equipment and vibration analysis now provides mechanics a tool for timely and effective monitoring of equipment health.
- PIP, RCM and condition monitoring training has been provided to the trades staff and has served as a good tool to anchor change.

Communications Plan

- Extensive commitment to regular communications of the program's progress, results and benefits have indicated to staff that it is not the "flavor of the month" initiative. Dialogue between all levels and staff involvement has increased significantly.
- Staff buy-in has been facilitated from timely program implementation of FAMP initiatives.
- Serving as a host site for Fortune 500 companies and other organizations has enabled change agents to solidify the program's goals and objectives and maintain momentum.

- The review and adoption of new metrics have engaged senior staff in the new program. Detailed research and discussions have led to the improvement of performance reporting to include leading and lagging indications, leading metrics help "drive" the program toward proactive maintenance and lagging metrics track progress. As shown in Table A-2, significant advancements have been made by the FAMP initiative.

Table A-2: DITP Metrics Comparison

Benchmark	DITP (2000)	DITP (2003)	Goal
Leading Indicators			
Operations Light Maintenance	0.5%	11%	10-15%
Preventive Maintenance	85%	91%	100%
Lagging Indicators			
Backlog (weeks)	7	5.2	4-6
Emergency Maintenance	<1%	< 1%	< 5%
Overtime	9%	5%	< 5%

CONCLUSION

An asset management program is a combination of tools and techniques whose success requires careful planning and a commitment of resources. This is a difficult task with pressures of normal workloads and competing corporate initiatives. Executive sponsorship and designated champions in each business unit, along with a road map or model and continuous communications at all organizational levels, can facilitate the change required to maintain a successful asset management program.

The overall objective of asset management is to put an optimal program in place that includes the use of industry best practices. To be successful and fully realize maximum benefit, all components need to be fully integrated and implemented in a comprehensive initiative. Key components, such as a maintenance strategy, CMMS, condition monitoring and materials management linked with training programs and a regular communications plan, have led industry leaders to world-class results.

The MWRA's research and drive to establish a complete and cost-effective asset management program has led to a model that can serve to assist other water quality utilities. The adoption of best practices will assist in protecting our ratepayers' investment, extending the life of our assets and facilitate our becoming more efficient and competitive in the changing world of privatization.

ACKNOWLEDGMENTS

These MWRA supporters have made it possible for the FAMP initiative to advance into a recognized, leading model for the water quality industry: Mike Hornbrook, Chief Operating Officer; John Vetere, Deer Island Director; Gerry Gallinaro, Deer Island Deputy Director - Maintenance and Dan O'Brien, Deer Island Capital Programs Manager.

Appendix B

Strategic Plan Worksheet Sample

Goal Area 1: Infrastructure & Equipment

#	Goal	#	Strategy	#	Action Items	Performance Measure	Target	Schedule
1	**Provide reliable infrastructure and high-quality, cost-effective utility services for collection and treatment of wastewater and stormwater.**	1.A	Continually align the Capital Improvement Program (CIP) Management Process with Best Management Practices (BMP's) to deliver timely, cost-effective projects.	1.A.1	Develop and implement a CIP planning workflow that involves stakeholders in a process that clearly defines customer needs and technical aspects for all projects.	% of Project where Planning Budget $ matches Construction Budget $	100%	January to June 2010
						Number scope changes in detailed design per project	0%	
				1.A.2	Develop and implement a Business Case review and approval process that includes Level of Service, Risk, Life Cycle Costing and Triple Bottom Line.	% of capital projects submitted to the CIP plan that receive a business case review	100%	January to September 2009 (Ready for 2010 CIP submittal)
				1.A.3	Develop and implement a design change management process and ensure projects are aligned with MSD design standards and stakeholder commentary.	% of review comments addressed	100%	July to December 2008
				1.A.4	Develop commissioning requirements and workflows for all asset classes, including a clear definition on "substantially complete".	% Asset classes with commissioning requirements	100%	January 2008 to September 2010
				1.A.5	Insert lessons learned concept into CIP workflows (planning, design, construction phases).	% of identified lessons learned addressed	100%	July to June 2009
				1.A.6	Support long term asset reliability by incorporating the RCM process in CIP projects.	% of assets that have a defined maintenance strategy at commissioning	100%	July 2008 to July 2009

Goal Area 1: Infrastructure & Equipment Continued

#	Goal	#	Strategy	#	Action Items	Performance Measure	Target	Schedule
		1.B	Improve stormwater, wastewater infrastructure, and fleet reliability.	1.B.1	Identify and categorize all assets including hierarchy development	% of assets categorized	100%	January to September 2010
						% of assets in hierarchy	100%	
				1.B.2	Develop and implement a risk model based on criticality, probability/likelihood of failure, asset performance, and cost criteria.	% of tasks to develop the model completed	100%	July 2008 to July 2009
				1.B.3	Perform high level (subjective) probability/likelihood of failure based on rules from risk model	% of assets in risk model	10%	July 2009 to December 2009
				1.B.4	Perform detailed level condition assessment utilizing data (ex. TV, vibration, oil analysis) and field assessments	% of assets in risk model	100%	July 2009 to January 2014
				1.B.5	Perform criticality assessment	% assets with criticality assessment complete	100%	January to December 2009

Appendix C

Executive Sponsor 360 Degree Review

EXECUTIVE SPONSOR 360 DEGREE REVIEW						
		Disagree				Agree
ART Topics:		**1**	**2**	**3**	**4**	**5**
1.0 ATTRIBUTES of an Executive Sponsor						
The **"Attributes"** of Executive Sponsorship (WHO) can be characterized by qualities such as:						
1.1	Good understanding of how the business operates and of the corporate strategy					
1.2	True stakeholder: can have a fundamental impact on the organization's performance					
1.3	Respected by peers with power to influence/impact success, overcome resistance					
1.4	In a position to authorize resources (short and long-term)					
1.5	Ability to provide guidelines to shape team decision making at all levels					
1.6	Ability to envision the future state; models and shapes others' behaviors					
1.7	Organized but not a micromanager					
1.8	Good communicator and storytelling skills with ability to motivate teams through good/bad times					
1.9	Availability to coach and mentor teams from kickoff to closure					
2.0 RESPONSIBILITIES of an Executive Sponsor						
The **"Responsibilities"** of Executive Sponsorship (WHAT) are defined as:						
2.1	Responsible for the business case evaluation (BCE) justification and overall success of the initiative					

EXECUTIVE SPONSOR 360 DEGREE REVIEW - Continued

2.2	Ensures goal alignment & communication with C-Suite including resource impacts by other initiatives					
2.3	Responsible for team member selection (including removals/ additions)					
2.4	Secures resources (funding, staff availability, outside support)					
2.5	Provides direction via team chartering and helps define critical success and risk factors					
2.6	Completes "Execution Readiness & Success Status" reviews including analysis and follow-up actions					
2.7	Responsible for securing buy-in from steering team; assures accountability, quality and timeliness					
2.8	Creates an environment where candid and honest dialog is the norm, challenges the status quo					
2.9	Establishes working relationship "guidelines" with project manager who manages scope/ budget/etc.					
2.10	Coordinates recognition/ celebration of success of team work efforts					
3.0 TOP 5 MODES of Success for an Executive Sponsor						
The **"Top 5 Success Modes"** of Executive Sponsorship (HOW) is built around the success **MODES** model on "daily activities" of an effective executive sponsor:						
3.1	**M**anage Cross-Functional Alignment – with executive peers, other initiatives, communicates across					

EXECUTIVE SPONSOR 360 DEGREE REVIEW - Continued

3.2	**O**wnership of the Business Case for Change – develops and owns BCE with project manager					
3.3	**D**irection and Leadership – charters steering team, monitors success/risk factors, active and visible					
3.4	**E**ncouragement and Resourcing – motivates, open/honest/ immediate feedback, assures resources					
3.5	**S**ustainment and Risk Management – team selection, owns "Execution Readiness & Success" reviews					

Appendix D
Team Charter Examples

Appendix C includes a team chartering overview, as well as two examples of team charters. One is for a steering team, the other for a maintenance task team.

TEAM CHARTERING OVERVIEW

What Is Chartering?

Chartering is a structured procedure used to guide a steering or task team through the process of defining itself, including its mission/objective; members; roles and responsibilities; work plan, including deliverables and schedule; expected benefits; and any other elements that give a team the clarity of purpose essential for becoming a high performing team. Examples include: operating principles, critical success factors, core values and quality performance. A chartering session is different from a conventional project "kickoff," in that kickoffs tend to focus on one-way communication of the "whats," such as milestones, deliverables, schedules, etc., whereas chartering uses two-way communications to engage team members and other participants to define the "hows" of the project, such as responsibilities, work plans, etc. A tangible product of this process is a written charter document that has been endorsed by all participants of the chartering session. A one page charter is recommended, but the maximum length should be no more than two pages.

What Are the Benefits of Chartering?

- Builds high levels of clarity, agreement and motivation among the participants at the beginning of a project
- Increases the probability that the team will be successful and achieve high quality performance

- Empowers team members, maximizing their effectiveness and influence
- Ensures better use of the collective resources and knowledge of the project team
- Provides means to monitor performance so problems can be elevated and corrective actions initiated
- Ensures team members share the same vision for the project
- Helps create team behaviors that are stronger than individual behaviors

What Is a Charter Document?

A written summary of the formal chartering elements for a project that includes, at a minimum, mission/objective, members, roles and responsibilities, work plan deliverables and schedule, and expected benefits. The charter document should be formally endorsed and shared with all individuals and groups who have primary interface and communications with the project team.

What Is a Chartering Element?

A chartering element is any of the possible topics that could be developed during the chartering process. These topics could be worked or discussed in a chartering session or included in the documented output of the chartering session. Here are definitions of possible chartering elements.

Definitions of Potential Charter Elements
Mission/Objective: Answers the questions: "Why does this project team exist?" "Why was it formed?" "What is it expected to do?" The mission/objective should be brief and clearly stated in a single sentence or short paragraph. The team mission/objective should be closely linked to the overall initiative's purpose or vision. In broad terms, the mission/objective is the organization's requirement of the project team. Often, the team's purpose has been created by the organization's management and is reviewed and refined in a chartering session.
Team Membership: The specific staff who will be members of the project team and defined in the chartering phase. These individuals must know why they are on the team and the scope of their membership in terms of roles, responsibilities, deliverables and length of commitment. Team members may be full-time or part-time. Membership, however, is different from providing expertise when requested or contributing at one or several meetings. Membership carries with it defined responsibilities and a degree of commitment to the team and the individual members of the team. Members are selected based on a number of criteria.
Roles and Responsibilities: The formal definition of functional roles and the scope of professional responsibility for the team members in which a specific result must be met. When a team sets clear collective and individual roles and responsibilities, it creates an environment in which every team member feels fully and personally accountable for project success. Since any team member's failure is likely to create a shortfall in achieving the team's goals, it is critical that every team member is accountable for the success of every other member.
Work Plan (Deliverables, Schedule): Defines the expected outcomes, such as deliverables and associated schedules, for project management teams, which is one of the most important elements. The greater the clarity of work plan details that align with the mission/objective increases the probability that the team will achieve success.
Expected Benefits: Defines a team's success in terms of results that are measurable against agreed upon criteria. Expected benefits may be established in terms of quantity, quality, time, cost, customer satisfaction, or a combination of these. These measures should align with the critical success factors of the project. The greater the clarity of the criteria, the greater the probability that team members, individually and collectively, will achieve them.

Definitions of Potential Charter Elements (Continued)
Critical Success Factors: Selected elements, usually between four and eight, that the project team believes are most crucial in achieving the purpose and scope of the project. Team members answer the question: What are the most important things we must accomplish to achieve success? Critical success factors are the vital aspects of the project that the project team must assure do not fail during implementation of the project plan. Failure to successfully address one of these factors can result in a failure of the project. These factors should be considered vital aspects of the project related to customer relations, team performance, project planning and project implementation. Performance measures should be created that align with each of the critical success factors.
Operating Principles: A set of guidelines that determine "how" the project team will perform the work of the project and govern itself. Guidelines are created to answer questions about how the team will make decisions, how it will create and measure goals, how it will communicate internally and externally, how it will resolve conflict and how it will manage change. By creating operating principles prior to implementation of detailed tasks, many potential problems can be avoided. Many of the operating principles can become the basis for certain work plan elements.
Core Values: Set the conditions that frame required behavior and also define the framework for decision-making and priority setting. If organizational values have been published, the team should review them and determine whether they are sufficiently descriptive for the team's circumstances and sufficient to describe team behavior. Under other circumstances, the team may want to work on its values specific to the team's mission. Core values set appropriate "sidebars" for acceptable actions and decisions.

ASSET MANAGEMENT PROGRAM

Steering Team Charter

Mission/Objective

The Facilities Asset Management Program (FAMP) Steering Team will provide oversight and guidance to the FAMP program as it relates to design and implementation of program elements across the organization.

Members

Name, Director
Name, Capital Programs
Name, Maintenance
Name, Operations
Name, Assistant Director
Name, Planning
Name, O&M Support
Name, Director
Name, O&M
Name, O&M
Name, Procurement
Name, Superintendent
Name, Finance

Executive Sponsor

Name, Chief Operating Officer

Deliverables and Schedule

1 Develop and implement program sustainment structure
2. Develop schedule and forum for updates to executive staff
3. Determine what support and organizational resources should be funded to support the FAMP program

Key Activities

- Attend monthly FAMP Joint Steering Committee/Project Team meetings
- Ensure appropriate staffing resources are assigned to the FAMP initiative
- Review and comment on consultant reports and in-house staff recommendations
- Attend and participate in quarterly forum events
- Attend task team meetings, as applicable
- Monitor progress of Master Asset Protection Plan (MAPP) schedule
- Provide quarterly FAMP updates to executive staff

Expected Benefits

- Timely implementation of FAMP program elements
- Agency-wide involvement and program communications
- Supports the goal of FAMP – integration of maintenance, operations, engineering and financing to optimally maintain Company X's assets to meet all regulatory requirements

Charter Date:

Signatures:

MAINTENANCE TEAM CHARTER

Mission/Objective

Establish and implement maintenance best practices, procedures, measures and continuous improvements, and share this knowledge with the entire staff to ensure business efficiency and continuity.

Team Leader:	Name	**Sponsor(s):**	Name
Facilitator:	(rotate)	**Scribe:**	Name

Team Members

Division	Team Members		Division	Team Members

Work Plan/Deliverables and Schedule

Task Description	Proposed Start Date	Estimated Completion Date
Gain common understanding of existing practices and maintenance leading practices within and outside the organization		
Charter, sponsor and monitor work efforts in these four focus areas:		
• **Inventory:** Status report and recommended actions to steering team		
• **RCM Training/Pilots for Critical Equipment:** Status report and recommended actions to steering team		
• **PM Job Plans:** Status report and recommended actions to steering team		
• **Metrics:** Status report and recommended actions to steering team		

Work Plan/Deliverables and Schedule (Continued)

Task Description	Proposed Start Date	Estimated Completion Date
Coordinate work activities with other AM teams, including CMMS, condition assessment, training, risk and levels of service; Attend and report progress at quarterly AM team forums		
Deliver maintenance initiative team status report and recommended actions to steering team		

Expected Benefits

- Increased knowledge, efficiency and implementation of maintenance best practices within the organization
- 'Ownership' by the organization's employees for identifying and implementing work process changes and continuous improvements
- Enhanced teamwork by improved communications and coordination of work processes
- Reduced lifecycle costs for the organization's assets and improved levels of service

Charter Date:

Endorsements:

Appendix E

Meeting Management Formats for Meeting Agenda and Meeting Minutes

MEETING AGENDA **Meeting Name Here**	**Date:** **Time/Duration:** **Location:**

Meeting Called By: List Name

Invited Parties: List Names and Organizations

Meeting Objectives (Examples below)

1. Introduce team members and present team's roles, responsibilities and expectations
2. Provide overview of project plan
3. Review and reach consensus on project and/or team charter
4. Provide opportunities for questions and input

Agenda Discussion Items

Topics	**Discussion Lead**
1. Welcome, introductions and overview of meeting objectives	John Fortin
2. Background/project purpose	List name(s)
3. Brief overview of asset management	List name(s)
4. High-level summary of project scope and schedule	List name(s)
5. Project chartering, including discussion of: a. Project roles, responsibilities and expectations b. Project governance/communications protocol, organizational chart c. Staff engagement and learning opportunities d. Input and feedback e. Signing of project charter	List name(s)
6. Wrap-up and final remarks	John Fortin

<table>
<tr><td>MEETING MINUTES
Meeting Name Here</td><td>Date:
Time/Duration:
Location:</td></tr>
<tr><td colspan="2">Meeting Called By: List Name</td></tr>
<tr><td colspan="2">Invited Parties: List Names and Organizations (Indicate invited versus those that actually attended)</td></tr>
<tr><td colspan="2">Meeting Objectives (Repeat from Agenda)</td></tr>
<tr><td colspan="2">Introduce team members and present team's roles, responsibilities and expectations</td></tr>
<tr><td colspan="2">Provide overview of project plan</td></tr>
<tr><td colspan="2">Review and reach consensus on project and/or team charter</td></tr>
<tr><td colspan="2">Provide opportunities for questions and input</td></tr>
<tr><td colspan="2">Meeting Minutes</td></tr>
<tr><td>Topics
(Repeat topics from Agenda)</td><td>Meeting Notes</td></tr>
<tr><td>1. Welcome, introductions and overview of meeting objectives</td><td>List focus area notes and follow-up activities, including name of owner (in bold font) and due date of follow-up activity</td></tr>
<tr><td>2. Background/project purpose</td><td>List focus area notes and follow-up activities, including name of owner (in bold font) and due date of follow-up activity</td></tr>
<tr><td>3. Brief overview of asset management</td><td>List focus area notes and follow-up activities, including name of owner (in bold font) and due date of follow-up activity</td></tr>
<tr><td>4. High-level summary of project scope and schedule</td><td>List focus area notes and follow-up activities, including name of owner (in bold font) and due date of follow-up activity</td></tr>
</table>

MEETING MINUTES - Continued

5. Project chartering, including discussion of: a. Project roles, responsibilities and expectations b. Project governance/ communications protocol, organizational chart c. Staff engagement and learning opportunities d. Input and feedback e. Signing of project charter	List focus area notes and follow-up activities, including **name of owner (in bold font)** and due date of follow-up activity
6. Wrap-up and final remarks	List focus area notes and follow-up activities, including **name of owner (in bold font)** and due date of follow-up activity Example: John Fortin noted the following action items at the conclusion of the meeting: 1) **Client project manager** to collect all signatures for project charter by <insert due date here>. 2) **John Fortin** to provide copies of referenced Reliabilityweb.com's asset management and reliability industry survey report by <insert due date here>.

Appendix F
Strategic Execution Readiness Review

STRATEGY EXECUTION READINESS ASSESSMENT						
		Disagree				Agree
Topic		1	2	3	4	5
1.0 Leadership						
1.1	There is a common vision for strategic change					
1.2	Leaders are committed to strategic change					
1.3	There is a strong sense of urgency for strategic change					
1.4	Leaders understand trust and respect each other					
1.5	Leaders are modeling new values and behaviors					
	Subtotal	0	0	0	0	0
2.0 Vision for Change						
2.1	The rationale for this strategic change is clear and compelling					
2.2	I have a clear understanding of the roadmap to achieve the vision					
2.3	I understand what this strategic change means for me					
2.4	I understand that this strategic change is good for the company					
2.5	I understand what I need to do to achieve the vision					
	Subtotal	0	0	0	0	0
3.0 Change Strategies						
3.1	There is clear authority and accountability for this strategic change process					
3.2	There is a clear project structure for keeping strategic change on track					
3.3	Problems that emerge will be dealt with effectively in a timely manner					
3.4	There is understanding of the issues involved and sufficient time has been allowed for the strategic change process					

Strategy Execution Readiness Assessment (Continued)

3.5	Related projects and initiatives will be well coordinated with this strategic change initiative					
	Subtotal	0	0	0	0	0
4.0 Overcoming Resistance to Change						
4.1	Managers have the skills needed to be successful at strategic change management					
4.2	There are rewards and recognition for participating in the initiative and consequences for not doing so					
4.3	There is all way communication on the strategic change initiative					
4.4	Everyone who will be impacted is clear on how strategic change affects them and what they need to do differently					
4.5	Staff will be given adequate training to achieve the new skills and behaviors to be successful					
	Subtotal	0	0	0	0	0
5.0 Staff Performance						
5.1	Company policies, rules and processes are being changed to support this initiative					
5.2	Change will be supported by current compensation, appraisal and career development processes					
5.3	The desired level of cross-functional cooperation is in place for this change to take place					
5.4	Staff will genuinely work to support this strategic change process rather than give the impression that they are supporting change					
5.5	Strategic change will be supported by current skill development processes (training programs, etc.)					
	Subtotal	0	0	0	0	0

Appendix G
Strategic Execution Status Review

EXECUTION SUCCESS STATUS REVIEW						
		Unacceptable			Exceptional	
Topics:		**1**	**2**	**3**	**4**	**5**
1.0 Communications						
1.1	Are communication activities being completed per the communication plan?					
1.2	Are we having positive and productive meetings?					
1.3	Are monthly status meetings providing necessary information to all parties? Are they conducted in an efficient and predictable manner?					
1.4	Are we providing each other with early notice of areas of concern? Are we being responsive to concerns raised by other parties?					
1.5	Are we improving?					
	Subtotal	0	0	0	0	0
2.0 Benefits Tracking						
2.1	Is the benefits tracking framework being completed on a timely basis?					
2.2	Are benefits and results realistic and auditable? (e.g. correlated to the original business case evaluation (BCE) estimates)					
2.3	Are benefits and results being communicated to all stakeholders?					
2.4	Are benefits and results being operationalized across the organization?					
2.5	Are we achieving program goals and objectives?					
	Subtotal	0	0	0	0	0

EXECUTION SUCCESS STATUS REVIEW - Continued

3.0 Project Management						
3.1	Project is within scope, budget and schedule?					
3.2	Project planning considers impact on the ongoing operations?					
3.3	Project administration is efficient? (e.g. monthly reports, invoicing, subcontractor involvement)					
3.4	Deliverables follow QA/QC plan?					
3.5	Are issues being addressed at the right levels in a timely manner?					
	Subtotal	0	0	0	0	0
4.0 Team Chartering						
4.1	Are teams being chartered in accordance with standard framework?					
4.2	Are we monitoring team performance against team charter guidelines?					
4.3	Are team charters consistent with project goals and objectives?					
4.4	Are steering team members providing guidance and mentoring?					
4.5	Is team performance improving?					
	Subtotal	0	0	0	0	0
5.0 Leading Change						
5.1	Is steering committee staff taking personal responsibility in leading change? (e.g. AM program is being discussed in staff meetings)					
5.2	Is cross-functional engagement being achieved?					

EXECUTION SUCCESS STATUS REVIEW - Continued

5.3	Are steering committee members leading change as opposed to reacting to change? (e.g. status quo being actively questioned)					
5.4	Is necessary stakeholder (including employees) involvement being achieved?					
5.5	Is a culture of continuous improvement taking root? (e.g. new practices/concepts are understood and being applied)					
	Subtotal	0	0	0	0	0
6.0 Training						
6.1	Is the training plan developed and being implemented?					
6.2	Is training linked to business practices and being documented/ made available for future use in the organization?					
6.3	Are employees learning new asset management skills?					
6.4	Is adequate knowledge transfer occurring? (e.g. consultant to our staff)					
6.5	Is impact of training being reflected in daily activities?					
	Subtotal	0	0	0	0	0

About the Author

John W. Fortin, CMRP, IAMC, LEED AP

Asset Management and Reliability Enthusiast

John Fortin is an asset management and reliability practitioner with over 30 years of facilities 'lifecycle' experience, including design, construction and operations and maintenance. He has developed and implemented effective organizational change management programs required to implement a sustainable asset management culture. John provides a practitioner's view to clients and through industry association events, shares his successes at designing and implementing the Facilities Asset Management Program for the Massachusetts Water Resources Authority at the 1,000 million gallon per day Deer Island Treatment Plant in Boston, Massachusetts. The award-winning project resulted in reduced costs, increased reliability and availability, and a shift from reactive to proactive work practices.

John is internationally recognized for his leadership in strategy development, implementation and change management approaches. He has led and today coaches and mentors cross-industry clients around the globe in the development and implementation of asset management and reliability best practices, some of which have won international awards. He utilizes proven and innovative techniques to provide sustainable change to clients' strategic programs and initiatives, which are now outlined in his DELTA FORCE and ART of Executive Sponsorship models.

As an industry leader, John enjoys working with a diverse group of people on their journey to world-class performance, leveraging his proven "execution" techniques and models that he has published for your use. May the DELTA FORCE be with you!

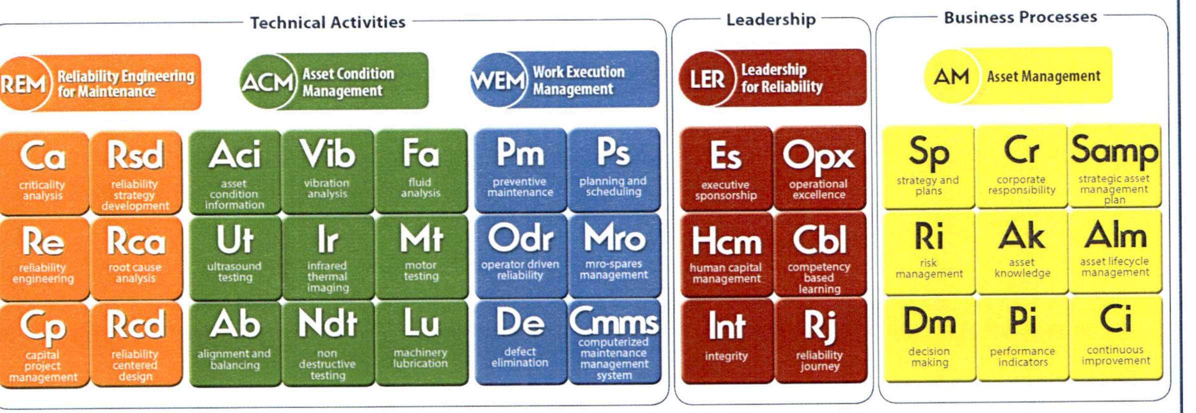

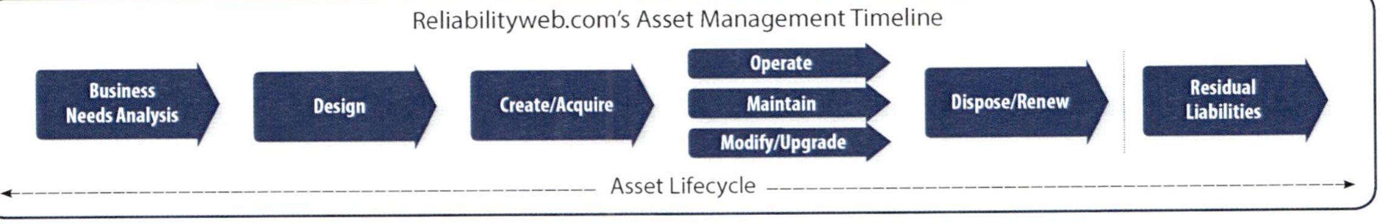

reliabilityweb.com • maintenance.org • reliabilityleadership.com

Reliabilityweb.com® and Uptime® Magazine Mission: **To make the people we serve safer and more successful.** One way we support this mission is to suggest a reliability system for asset performance management as pictured above. Our use of the Uptime Elements is designed to assist you in categorizing and organizing your own Body of Knowledge (BoK) whether it be through training, articles, books or webinars. Our hope is to make YOU safer and more successful.

ABOUT RELIABILITYWEB.COM

Created in 1999, Reliabilityweb.com provides educational information and peer-to-peer networking opportunities that enable safe and effective reliability and asset management for organizations around the world.

ACTIVITIES INCLUDE:

Reliabilityweb.com® (www.reliabilityweb.com) includes educational articles, tips, video presentations, an industry event calendar and industry news. Updates are available through free email subscriptions and RSS feeds. **Confiabilidad.net** is a mirror site that is available in Spanish at www.confiabilidad.net.

Uptime® Magazine (www.uptimemagazine.com) is a bi-monthly magazine launched in 2005 that is highly prized by the reliability and asset management community. Editions are obtainable in both print and digital.

Reliability Leadership Institute® Conferences and Training Events (www.reliabilityleadership.com) offer events that range from unique, focused-training workshops and seminars to small focused conferences to large industry-wide events, including the International Maintenance Conference (IMC), MaximoWorld and The RELIABILITY Conference™ (TRC).

MRO-Zone Bookstore (www.mro-zone.com) is an online bookstore offering a reliability and asset management focused library of books, DVDs and CDs published by Reliabilityweb.com.

Association of Asset Management Professionals (www.maintenance.org) is a member organization and online community that encourages professional development and certification and supports information exchange and learning with 50,000+ members worldwide.

A Word About Social Good

Reliabilityweb.com is mission-driven to deliver value and social good to the reliability and asset management communities. *Doing good work and making profit is not inconsistent*, and as a result of Reliabilityweb.com's mission-driven focus, financial stability and success has been the outcome. For over a decade, Reliabilityweb.com's positive contributions and commitment to the reliability and asset management communities have been unmatched.

Other Causes

Reliabilityweb.com has financially contributed to include industry associations, such as SMRP, AFE, STLE, ASME and ASTM, and community charities, including the Salvation Army, American Red Cross, Wounded Warrior Project, Paralyzed Veterans of America and the Autism Society of America. In addition, we are proud supporters of our U.S. Troops and first responders who protect our freedoms and way of life. That is only possible by being a for-profit company that pays taxes.

I hope you will get involved with and explore the many resources that are available to you through the Reliabilityweb.com network.

Warmest regards,
Terrence O'Hanlon
CEO, Reliabilityweb.com